*f*P

Also by William Deresiewicz

*A Jane Austen Education: How Six Novels Taught Me About Love, Friendship, and the Things That Really Matter*

# EXCELLENT SHEEP

*The Miseducation of the American Elite
and the Way to a Meaningful Life*

## WILLIAM DERESIEWICZ

FREE PRESS
*New York London Toronto Sydney New Delhi*

Portions of this book have appeared in different form in the *American Scholar,* the *Nation,* and the *Chronicle of Higher Education.*

FREE PRESS
A Division of Simon & Schuster, Inc.
1230 Avenue of the Americas
New York, NY 10020

First Free Press hardcover edition August 2014

FREE PRESS and colophon are trademarks of Simon & Schuster, Inc.

For information about special discounts for bulk purchases, please contact Simon & Schuster Special Sales at 1-866-506-1949 or business@simonandschuster.com.

The Simon & Schuster Speakers Bureau can bring authors to your live event. For more information or to book an event, contact the Simon & Schuster Speakers Bureau at 1-866-248-3049 or visit our website at www.simonspeakers.com.

*Interior design by Aline Pace*
*Jacket design by Olivia Munday*

Manufactured in the United States of America

10 9 8 7 6 5

Library of Congress Cataloging-in-Publication Data
Deresiewicz, William, 1964–
    Excellent sheep : the miseducation of the American elite and the way to a meaningful life / William Deresiewicz.
        pages cm
    1. Education, Higher—United States. 2. Universities and colleges—United States. 3. Elite (Social sciences)—Education—United States. 4. Critical thinking—Study and teaching (Higher)—United States. 5. Reasoning—Study and teaching (Higher)—United States. 6. Education, Higher—Aims and objectives—United States. 7. Education, Higher—Social aspects—United States. I. Title.
    LA227.4.D74 2014
    378.73—dc23

                                                                    2014010790

ISBN 978-1-4767-0271-1
ISBN 978-1-4767-0273-5 (ebook)

*For my students*
*and as always, for Jill*

# Contents

# Introduction

This book, in many ways, is a letter to my twenty-year-old self. It talks about the kinds of things I wish that someone had encouraged me to think about when I was going to college—such as what the point of college might be in the first place.

I was like so many kids today (and so many kids back then). I went off to college like a sleepwalker, like a zombie. College was a blank. College was the "next thing." You went to college, you studied something, and afterward you went on to the next next thing, most probably some kind of graduate school. Up ahead were vaguely understood objectives: status, wealth, getting to the top—in a word, "success." As for where you went to school, that was all about bragging rights, so of course you chose the most prestigious place that let you in. What it meant to actually get an education, and why you might want one—how it could help you acquire a self, or develop an independent mind, or find your way in the world—all this was off the table. Like kids today, I was processed through a system everyone around me simply took for granted.

I started college in 1981. The system, then, was in its early days, but it was already, unmistakably, a system, a set of tightly interlocking parts. When I speak in this book of elite education, I mean prestigious institutions like Harvard or Stanford or Williams as well as the larger universe of second-tier selective schools, but I also mean everything that leads up to and away from them: the private and affluent public high schools; the ever-growing industry of tutors and consultants, test-prep courses and enrichment programs; the admissions process itself, squatting like a dragon at the entrance to adulthood; the brand-name graduate schools and employment opportunities that come after the BA; and the parents and communities, largely upper middle class, who push their children into the maw of this machine. In short, our entire system of elite education.

What that system does to kids and how they can escape from it, what it does to our society and how we can dismantle it—those are the subjects of this book. I was teaching a class at Yale on the literature of friendship. One day we got around to talking about the importance of being alone. The ability to engage in introspection, I suggested, is the essential precondition for living the life of the mind, and the essential precondition for introspection is solitude. My students took this in for a second—introspection, solitude, the life of the mind, things they probably had not been asked to think about before—then one of them said, with a dawning sense of self-awareness, "So are you saying that we're all just, like, really excellent sheep?"

All? Surely not. But after twenty-four years in the Ivy League—college at Columbia; a PhD at the same institution, including five years as a graduate instructor; and ten years, altogether, on the faculty at Yale—that was more or less how I had come to feel about it. The system manufactures students who are smart and talented and driven, yes, but also anxious, timid, and lost, with little intellectual curiosity and a stunted sense of purpose: trapped in a bubble of privilege, heading meekly in the same direction, great at what they're doing but with no idea why they're doing it. In 2008, on my way out the door, I published an essay that sketched out a few of these criticisms. Titled "The Disadvantages of an Elite Education," the article appeared in the *American Scholar,* a small literary quarterly. At best, I thought, it might get a few thousand readers.

Instead, it started to go viral almost from the moment it came out. Within a few weeks, the piece had been viewed a hundred thousand times (with many times that number in the months and years to come). Apparently I'd touched a nerve. These were not just the grumblings of an ex-professor. As it turned out from the many emails I began to get, the vast majority from current students and recent graduates, I had evoked a widespread discontent among today's young high achievers—a sense that the system was cheating them out of a meaningful education, instilling them with values they rejected but couldn't somehow get beyond, and failing to equip them to construct their futures.

Since then I have spoken with students on campuses across the country, corresponded with many others, answered these young people's questions and asked my own, and heard and read their stories. It has been an education in itself, and this book is a reflection of that ongoing dialogue. Where possible, I've used their words to help me talk about the issues we've discussed, but every page has been informed by my sense of what these kinds of students need and want to think about. A lot of books get published about higher education, but none, as far as I can tell, are speaking to students themselves— still less, listening to them.

I begin the book by discussing the system itself—one that, to put it in a nutshell, forces you to choose between learning and success. Education is the way that a society articulates its values: the way that it transmits its values. While I'm often critical of the sort of kids who populate selective schools, my real critique is aimed at the adults who've made them who they are—that is to say, at the rest of us. Part 2 begins to explain what students can do, as individuals, to rescue themselves from the system: what college should be for, how to find a different kind of path in life, what it means to be a genuine leader. Part 3 extends the argument, talking in detail about the purpose of a liberal arts education, the value of the humanities, and the need for dedicated teachers and small classrooms. My aim is not to tell young people where to go to school so much as why.

Part 4 returns to the larger social question. The system is charged with producing our leadership class, the so-called meritocracy—the people who run our institutions, governments, and corporations. So how has that been going? Not, it's clear by now, too well. What we're doing to our kids we're ultimately doing to ourselves. The time has long since passed, I argue, to rethink, reform, and reverse the entire project of elite education.

A word on what I mean when I speak of the elite. I don't intend the term as it is often now deployed, as a slur against liberals, intellectuals, or anyone who disagrees with Bill O'Reilly, but simply as a name for those who occupy the upper echelons of our society: conservatives as well as liberals, businesspeople as well as professionals, the upper and the upper middle classes both—the managers, the winners, the whole cohort of people who went to selective colleges and are running society for their own exclusive benefit. This book is also, implicitly, a portrait of that class, whose time to leave the stage of history has now so evidently come.

# PART 1

*Sheep*

# One

## The Students

"Super People," the writer James Atlas has called them—the stereo-typical ultra-high-achieving elite college students of today. A double major, a sport, a musical instrument, a couple of foreign languages, service work in distant corners of the globe, a few hobbies thrown in for good measure: they have mastered them all, and with an apparent effortlessness, a serene self-assurance, that leaves adults and peers alike in awe. Today's elite students, says David Brooks, project a remarkable level of "comfort, confidence, and competence." In Jonathan Franzen's novel *Freedom*, the kids at a prestigious liberal arts college "seemed cheerfully competent at everything."

Such is our image of these enviable youngsters, who appear to be the winners in the race we have made of childhood. But the reality—as I have witnessed it among my former students, heard about it from the hundreds of young people who have written to me over the last few years or whom I have met on campuses across the country, and read about it in places where these kids confide their feelings—is something very different. Look beneath the façade of affable confidence and seamless well-adjustment that today's elite students have learned to project, and what you often find are toxic levels of fear, anxiety, and depression, of emptiness and aimlessness and isolation. We all know about the stressed-out, overpressured high school student; why do we assume that things get better once she gets to college?

The evidence says they do not. A large-scale survey of college freshmen recently found that self-reports of emotional well-being have fallen to their lowest level in the twenty-five-year history of the study. In another recent survey—summarized by the American Psychological Association under the headline "The Crisis on Campus"—nearly half of college students reported feelings of hopelessness, while almost a third spoke of feeling "so depressed that it was difficult to function during the past 12 months." College counseling services are being overwhelmed. Utilization rates have been climbing since the mid-1990s, and among the students who show up, the portion with severe psychological problems has nearly tripled, to almost half. Convening a task force on student mental health in 2006, Stanford's provost wrote that "increasingly, we are seeing students struggling with mental health concerns ranging from self-esteem issues and developmental disorders to depression, anxiety, eating disorders, self-mutilation behaviors, schizophrenia and suicidal behavior." As a college president wrote me, "we appear to have an epidemic of depression among younger people."

If anything, the already dire situation in high school deteriorates further in college, as students suddenly find themselves on their own, trying to negotiate an overwhelming new environment and responsible for making decisions about their future that their childhood has left them unequipped to handle. An increasing number cope by going on antidepressants or antianxietals (not to mention relying on stimulants like Adderall to help them handle the pressure); others by taking leaves of absence—or at least, by dreaming about it. "If the wheels are going to come off," a Pomona student has put it, "it's going to be in college."

I have heard about this kind of misery again and again. From a graduate instructor at Princeton: "I just had an undergrad thesis-student faint in my office the other day because she was feeling so much pressure from her academic life." From someone who was in the process of transferring out of Stanford: "For many students, rising to the absolute top means being consumed by the system. I've seen my peers sacrifice health, relationships, exploration, activities that can't be quantified and are essential for developing souls and hearts, for grades and resume building." From a student at Yale: "A friend of mine said it nicely: 'I might be miserable, but were I not miserable, I wouldn't be at Yale.'"

Isolation is a major factor. "People at Yale," a former student said, "do not have time for real relationships." Another told me that she didn't have friends in college until she learned to slow down a little senior year, that going out to a movie was a novel experience at that point. A recent article in *Harvard Magazine* described students passing their suitemates like ships in the night as they raced from one activity to another. Kids know how to network and are often good at "people skills," but those are very different things from actual friendship. Romantic life is conducted in an equally utilitarian spirit: hookups or friends with benefits to scratch the sexual itch, "pragmantic" "college marriages," as Ross Douthat puts it, that provide stability and enable partners to place career first. "I positioned myself in college in such a way," said a University of Pennsylvania student who was recently quoted in the *New York Times*, "that I can't have a meaningful romantic relationship, because I'm always busy and the people that I am interested in are always busy, too."

But the compulsive overachievement of today's elite college students—the sense that they need to keep running as fast as they can—is not the only thing that keeps them from forming the deeper relationships that might relieve their anguish. Something more insidious is operating, too: a resistance to vulnerability, a fear of looking like the only one who isn't capable of handling the pressure. These are young people who have always succeeded at everything, in part by projecting the confidence that they always will. Now, as they get to college, the stakes are higher and the competition fiercer. Everybody thinks that they're the only one who's suffering, so nobody says anything, so everybody suffers. Everyone feels like a fraud; everyone thinks that everybody else is smarter than they are.

Students at Stanford talk about "Stanford Duck Syndrome": serene on the surface, paddling madly underneath. In a recent post titled "Meltdown" on an MIT student website, a sophomore confessed her feelings of shame and worthlessness and often "overwhelming loneliness." The post went viral, eliciting recognition and gratitude from students at at least a dozen other schools. "Thank you for sharing," said one comment. "We all feel this way more often than we would care to admit. Thank you for being brave enough to put this into words." Students at Pomona, which prides itself on being ranked the "fourth-happiest" college in America (whatever that means), have told me of the burden that comes with that very self-image, as well as from the regimen of group activities with which the college seeks to reinforce it: the pressure that they feel to satisfy the happiness police by projecting an appearance of perfect well-being.

Isolated from their peers, these kids are also cut off from themselves. The endless hoop-jumping, starting as far back as grade school, that got them into an elite college in the first place—the clubs, bands, projects, teams, APs, SATs, evenings, weekends, summers, coaches, tutors, "leadership," "service"—left them no time, and no tools, to figure out what they want out of life, or even out of college. Questions of purpose and passion were not on the syllabus. Once they've reached the shining destination toward which their entire childhood and adolescence had been pointed, once they're through the gates at Amherst or Dartmouth, many kids find out that they have no idea why they're there, or what they want to do next.

As Lara Galinsky, the author of *Work on Purpose,* expressed it to me, young people are not trained to pay attention to the things they feel connected to. "You cannot say to a Yalie 'find your passion,'" a former student wrote me. "Most of us do not know how and that is precisely how we arrived at Yale, by having a passion only for success." According to Harry R. Lewis, a former dean of Harvard College, "Too many students, perhaps after a year or two spent using college as a treadmill to nowhere, wake up in crisis, not knowing why they have worked so hard." One young woman at Cornell summed up her life to me like this: "I hate all my activities, I hate all my classes, I hated everything I did in high school, I expect to hate my job, and this is just how it's going to be for the rest of my life."

If adults are unaware of all this, that's partly because they're looking in the wrong direction. Getting A's no longer means that everything's okay, assuming that it ever did. "We have students, who, no matter what else is going on in their lives, know how to get those grades," Rabbi Patricia Karlin-Neumann, Stanford's university chaplain, has said. "It's important for us to take away the blinders that keep us from seeing their distress."

Mainly, though, these kids are very good at hiding their problems from us. I was largely unaware myself, during my years at Yale, of the depth of my students' unhappiness. Only now that I am no longer in a position of authority do some of them feel comfortable enough to open up. The student who told me that she had no friends until her senior year had seemed, if anything, unusually healthy: funny, friendly, "real," not obnoxiously competitive or on the make, and a brilliant student, to boot. Another kid, equally great, equally well-adjusted for all that I could see, later confessed that she'd been miserable in college, depressed or stressed-out all the time. By the time they finish high school—after years of learning how to please their teachers and coaches, not to mention schmoozing with their parents' friends—elite students have become accomplished adult-wranglers. Polite, pleasant, mild, and presentable; well-mannered, well-groomed, and well-spoken (not to mention, often enough, well-medicated), they have fashioned that façade of happy, healthy high achievement.

**It would be bad enough** if all this misery were being inflicted for the sake of genuine learning, but that is quite the opposite of what the system now provides. Our most prestigious colleges and universities love to congratulate themselves on the caliber of their incoming students: their average SAT scores, the proportion that comes from the top 10 percent of their high school class, the narrowness of the admissions sieve that lets them in, all the numbers *U.S. News & World Report* has taught us to worship. And make no mistake; today's elite students are, in purely academic terms, phenomenally well prepared.

How could they not be, given how carefully they're bred, how strenuously sorted and groomed? They are the academic equivalent of all-American athletes, coached and drilled and dieted from the earliest years of life. Whatever you demand of them, they'll do. Whatever bar you place in front of them, they'll clear. A friend who teaches at a top university once asked her class to memorize thirty lines of the eighteenth-century poet Alexander Pope. Every single kid got every single line correct, down to the punctuation marks. Seeing them write out the exercise in class, she said, was a thing of wonder, like watching Thoroughbreds circle a track.

The problem is that students have been taught that that is all that education is: doing your homework, getting the answers, acing the test. Nothing in their training has endowed them with the sense that something larger is at stake. They've learned to "be a student," not to use their minds. I was talking with someone who teaches at a branch campus of a state university. His students don't think for themselves, he complained. Well, I said, Yale students think for themselves, but only because they know we want them to. I taught many wonderful young people during my years in the Ivy League— bright, thoughtful, creative kids whom it was a pleasure to talk with and learn from. But most of them seemed content to color within the lines that their education had marked out for them. Very few were passionate about ideas. Very few saw college as part of a larger project of intellectual discovery and development, one that they directed by themselves and for themselves.

I am far from alone in this perception. A friend who taught at Amherst mentioned a student who came to her for extra help with his writing—but only because he had already been admitted to medical school and now felt free to actually learn. If he were a freshman or sophomore, he said, he wouldn't have taken the time. Another friend teaches fine arts at a prestigious liberal arts college. His kids are eager to accept creative challenges, he's told me, but only as long as it will help them get an A. "I cannot imagine a Yale undergraduate spending an entire weekend lying in bed reading poetry or glued to a keyboard writing a breakthrough iPhone app," said a former colleague in the computer science department, who went to college in the late 1970s. "Yet, when I was an undergraduate, people did things like that all the time; passionate weirdos were all over the place, and they were part of what made college interesting."

Students simply don't have time for that kind of headlong immersion. The frenzy of extracurricular activities has expanded to fill the available space, displacing intellectual pursuits as the focus of student energy. David Brooks and other observers have spoken about the death of the late-night bull session, the scarcity of spontaneous intellectual discussion. I've heard similar complaints from students at Brown, Penn, Cornell, Pomona, and Columbia. "I've never been able to justify to myself why I feel so much 'smarter'—more productive, more creative, more interesting (and more importantly, more interested)—during the summers than I ever do during the school year," a Princeton senior wrote me. A young woman from another school told me this about her boyfriend at Yale:

> Before he started college, he spent most of his time reading and writing short stories. Three years later, he's painfully insecure, worrying about things my public-educated friends don't give a second thought to, like the stigma of eating lunch alone and whether he's "networking" enough. No one but me knows he fakes being well-read by thumbing through the first and last chapters of any book he hears about and obsessively devouring reviews in lieu of the real thing. He does this not because he's incurious, but because there's a bigger social reward for being able to talk about books than for actually reading them.

There are exceptions, of course: seekers, thinkers, "passionate weirdos," kids who approach the work of the mind with a pilgrim spirit, who insist, against all odds, on trying to get a real education. But their experience in college tends to make them feel like freaks. "Yale," one of them said, "is not conducive to searchers." Another said, about a friend of hers who'd transferred out, "She found Yale stifling to the parts of yourself that you'd call a soul." Said a third, "It's hard to build your soul when everyone around you is trying to sell theirs."

My examples tend to come from Yale, since that is mainly where I taught, but I do not mean to single out that institution. If anything, I think it probably deserves its reputation as the best among elite universities (as distinct from liberal arts colleges) at nurturing creativity and intellectual independence. Notoriously pre-professional places like Penn, Duke, or Washington University, or notoriously anti-intellectual ones like Princeton or Dartmouth, are clearly far worse. But that's precisely what's so frightening. If Yale is the best, then the best is pretty bad.

Yet if I have learned one thing in the last few years, it is that today's elite students do not arrive in college as a herd of sheep or army of robots, with a few rebel intellectuals off at the edges. Most of them are somewhere in the middle: idealistic and curious, like kids before them, hungry for purpose and meaning, like kids before them, but beset by psychological demands that are inevitable products of the process that propelled them into college in the first place.

"Every educational system," wrote Allan Bloom, "wants to produce a certain kind of human being." Growing up elite means learning to value yourself in terms of the measures of success that mark your progress into and through the elite: the grades, the scores, the trophies. That is what you're praised for; that is what you are rewarded for. Your parents brag; your teachers glow; your rivals grit their teeth.

Finally, the biggest prize of all, the one that draws a line beneath your adolescence and sums you up for all the world to see: admission to the college of your dreams. Or rather, not finally—because the game, of course, does not end there. College is naturally more of the same. Now the magic terms are GPA, Phi Beta Kappa, Fulbright, MCAT, Harvard Law, Goldman Sachs. They signify not just your fate, but your identity; not just your identity, but your value. They are *who* you are, and what you're worth.

The result is what we might refer to as credentialism. The purpose of life becomes the accumulation of gold stars. Hence the relentless extracurricular busyness, the neglect of learning as an end in itself, the inability to imagine doing something that you can't put on your resume. Hence the constant sense of competition. (If you want to increase participation in an activity, a Stanford professor told me, make entry to it competitive.) Hence the endemic academic corner-cutting that Douthat describes in *Privilege*, a memoir of his time at Harvard, where all that intellect is put to the service, not of learning as much as possible, but of getting away with doing as little as you can. Hence the vogue for double majors. It isn't enough anymore to take a bunch of electives in addition to your primary focus, to roam freely across the academic fields, making serendipitous connections and discoveries, the way that American higher education was designed (uniquely, among the world's systems) to allow you to do. You have to get that extra certification now, or what has it all been for? I even met a quadruple major once. He seemed to think it meant that he was very smart.

With credentialism comes a narrow practicality that's capable of understanding education only in terms of immediate utility, and that marches, at the most prestigious schools, beneath a single banner: economics. In 1995, economics was the most popular major at three of the top ten universities or top ten liberal arts colleges on the most recent lists in *U.S. News*. In 2013, it was the biggest at a minimum of eight and as many as fourteen. Among the universities, it was the biggest at Harvard, Princeton, Penn, Dartmouth, and probably Columbia and the University of Chicago (determinations are sometimes difficult because of changes in reporting). It was the biggest at four of the top ten liberal arts colleges, places that are supposed to be about a different sort of education—Williams, Middlebury, Pomona, and Claremont McKenna—and probably also at Amherst, Swarthmore, Carleton, and Wellesley. It was almost as popular among the next ten schools on each list, the rest of the top twenty, representing the largest major at as many as six of the universities and six more of the colleges, for a grand total of 26 of the 40 schools on the two lists combined. Sixty-five percent, for just a single major: a stunning convergence.

Meanwhile, not coincidentally, finance and consulting have emerged as the most coveted careers. In 2007, about half of Harvard seniors who had full-time jobs lined up for after graduation were going into one of those two industries. The numbers softened a bit after the financial collapse, but not by much and not for long. By 2010, nearly half of Harvard graduates were still going into one of those fields, as well as more than half of those at Penn and more than a third at Cornell, Stanford, and MIT. In 2011, 36 percent of Princeton graduates went into finance alone.

At Yale it was only about a quarter, between the two fields, in 2010, but as junior Marina Keegan put it the following year, in an essay that went viral on the Web, why should that be "only"? "In a place as diverse and disparate as Yale, it's remarkable that such a large percentage of people are doing anything the same—not to mention something as significant as their postgraduate plans." And it is all the more remarkable, she went on, given that students arrive at college innocent of either intention. "I conducted a credible and scientific study . . . earlier this week—asking freshman after freshman what they thought they might be doing upon graduation. Not one of them said they wanted to be a consultant or an investment banker."

**The question, then, is why.** Why do so many elite students end up choosing one of those two fields, and what does that tell us about their peer group as a whole? Greed alone is not the explanation. Remember that these kids have been conditioned, above all, to jump through hoops. That's what feels familiar; that's what feels safe; that's what feels like the right thing to do. In high school, everybody had the same objective, to get into the most prestigious college possible, and the hoops were all lined up to lead you there. But once you get to college, things are not so certain anymore. Directions multiply, and many of the paths are foggy. As Keegan suggested, being a musician does not have an application form. How do you become a social entrepreneur, a politician, a screenwriter? How do you get to work at the State Department, in Silicon Valley, for the *New York Times*? How many options are there that you haven't even heard of, and how does getting a job work, anyway? It isn't any wonder, as graduation draws near, that a lot of students scurry frantically around, looking for another hoop to jump through.

And speaking of options, these kids have all been told that theirs are limitless. Once you commit to something, though, that ceases to be true. A former student sent me an essay he wrote, a few years after college, called "The Paradox of Potential." Yale students, he said, are like stem cells. They can be anything in the world, so they try to delay for as long as possible the moment when they have to become just one thing in particular. Possibility, paradoxically, becomes limitation. "My friends and I didn't run sprinting down a thousand career paths, bound for all corners of the globe," he wrote. "Instead, we moved cautiously, in groups, plodding down a few well-worn trails so as to ensure that two or four years down the road, we could be stem cells again, still undifferentiated, still brimming with potential."

That's the situation that consulting firms, especially, have learned to exploit. Their recruiters descend upon elite campuses in force. They make it easy to apply—but they also make it hard to get selected, which is even better. The job looks great on your resume, and you aren't foreclosing any options, since you can still do anything you want to after you leave. As for the work itself, it's pretty much like college: rigorous analysis, integration of disparate forms of information, clear and effective communication. You don't even have to have studied economics; firms are often happy to hire humanities majors. They're looking only for exactly what the colleges were: intelligence, diligence, energy—aptitude. And of course, they offer you a lot of money.

A former student wrote me this:

*The real problem is that Yalies and our peers now feel like they're somehow wasting their degree by taking a job that doesn't pay 100K the first year, or ever. I think consulting in particular appeals to this perverse fantasy that most Ivy Leaguers harbor deep down inside, which is that someone should pay them for simply having gone to Yale or Harvard or wherever. All of the various reasons I've been given by my peers to explain why they're consulting next year boil down to the same thing: "because I can." Few people have the balls to walk away from that.*

Nor is it consulting firms alone. Most of what is true of them is also true of the investment banks. "What Wall Street figured out," another student wrote me, "is that colleges are producing a large number of very smart, completely confused graduates. Kids who have ample mental horsepower, an incredible work ethic and no idea what to do next." Nor is law school essentially different, even if the financial rewards are delayed for several years. Nor, in many ways, is Teach For America, by far the most popular postgraduate destination among the nonprofits: heavy recruitment, clear path, competitive application process, limited time commitment, looks great on your resume, doesn't foreclose options, very impressive, another gold star—and you can always do Bain or Morgan afterward, as some alumni of the program do. TFA is worlds away from Wall Street, morally speaking, but the overriding problem, when it comes to the kinds of choices that elite students make after college, is not greed; it is inertia. If love of money tends to win out, that is largely because so many kids leave college without a sense of inner purpose—in other words, of what else might be worth their time.

**The irony, then, is this.** Elite students are told that they can be whatever they want, but most of them end up choosing to be one of a few very similar things. Whole fields have disappeared from view: the clergy, the military, electoral politics, teaching, even academia itself, for the most part, including basic science. It is true that today's young people appear to be more socially engaged, as a whole, than kids have been for several decades: more concerned about the state of the world and more interested in trying to do something about it. It is true, as well, that they are more apt to harbor creative or entrepreneurial impulses. But it is also true, at least at the most selective schools, that even if those aspirations make it out of college—a very big "if"—they tend to be played out within the same narrow conception of what constitutes a valid life: affluence, credentials, and prestige.

What I saw at Yale I have continued to see at campuses around the country. Everybody looks extremely normal, and everybody looks the same. No hippies, no punks, no art school types or hipsters, no butch lesbians or gender queers, no black kids in dashikis. The geeks don't look that geeky; the fashionable kids go in for understated elegance. Everyone dresses as if they're ready to be interviewed at a moment's notice. You're *young,* I want to say to them. Take a *chance* with yourselves. Never mind "diversity." What we're getting is thirty-two flavors of vanilla. I am not lamenting a bygone era of student rebellion; college used to be understood as a time to experiment with different selves, of whatever type. Now students all seem to be converging on the same self, the successful upper-middle-class professional, impersonating the adult they've already decided they want to become. "However much diversity Yale's freshman classes may have," a former student wrote, "its senior classes have far less."

Everybody does the same thing because everybody's doing the same thing. A former student talked to me about the "salmon run." A University of Michigan graduate spoke of the "conveyor belt." The operative principle is known as triangular desire: wanting something because you see that other people want it and assume that it must be valuable. "There was," wrote Michael Lewis about the salmon run of his own day, "a sense of safety in numbers."

The key word there is "safety." Beneath the other factors—the entitlement, the lack of direction, the desire not to close down options—the force that drives the salmon run is fear. It is the exact fear (and more than fear: the panic, the often crippling anxiety) that lies behind that façade of serene achievement that elite college students learn to show the world. So extreme are the admission standards now, so ferocious the competition, that kids who manage to get into elite colleges have, by definition, never experienced anything but success. The prospect of *not* being successful terrifies them, disorients them, defeats them. They have been haunted their whole lives by a fear of failure—often, in the first instance, by their parents' fear of failure. The cost of falling short, even temporarily, becomes not merely practical, but existential.

The result is a violent aversion to risk. You have no margin for error, so you avoid the possibility that you will ever make an error. That is one of the reasons that elite education has become so inimical to learning. As Harry R. Lewis, the former Harvard dean, has written, nobody wants to take a chance on a class they might not ace, so nobody is willing to venture beyond the things they already know and do very well. Experimenting, exploring, discovering new ways to look at the world as well as new capacities within yourself—the things a college education is supposed to be about—fall by the wayside. Nobody wants to let any of the dozen balls they're juggling drop; nobody wants to lag behind in the credentials race. When a student at Pomona told me that she'd love to have a chance to think about the things she's studying, only she doesn't have the time, I asked her if she had ever considered not trying to get an A in every class. She looked at me as if I had made an indecent suggestion.

**Senior year is when this** training in playing it safe meets the need to start making real decisions about your life, and that large population of kids in the middle begins to assume the shape of a herd. Remember what my student said before, about how difficult it is to make a different choice. And that's before you start to see that everybody else is making the *same* choice. Many kids have spoken to me, as they navigated their senior years, about the pressure they felt from their peers—from their *peers*—to justify a different kind of life. You're made to feel like you're crazy, they've told me: crazy to forsake the sure thing, crazy to think it could work, crazy to imagine that you even have a right to try.

Nor does graduation make these issues go away. While some kids make a choice and don't look back—for good or ill, whether they have chosen from conviction or desperation—many continue to struggle with all the same feelings and pressures. I have seen students stumble for years, as many bright young people do today, unwilling to submit to doing something that they can't feel passionate about but still not knowing where their passion really lies. One spoke of continuing to struggle not only with anxiety and fear, but also with ambition: not, that is, with a genuine desire for excellence, but with the feeling of being a failure if you don't continue to amass the blue-chip names, the need to keep on doing the most prestigious possible thing—and the constant awareness, over your shoulder, of all the prestigious things that your former classmates are doing.

Another student went to work some years ago for a consulting firm. He used to look me up every once in a while when he came back to campus on recruiting trips. Every time I saw him, he would tell me that he wanted to get out and do something creative instead, something meaningful, but that he didn't know how, any longer, because he couldn't imagine surrendering the lifestyle to which he had become accustomed. In other words—I have heard this a lot—he'd become addicted to the money.

Yet another recent graduate, a talented writer who *is* sticking by her guns, and who had always been indifferent to the race for wealth and status, wrote me this:

*Every day, I fight a compulsion to find a good ladder and scurry up it for the next fifteen years, because I can tell from the dread in my gut that this is the wrong thing to do. If I became a senior editor at the* New Yorker *without having taken a circuitous and ultimately interesting route, I would be unhappy. And yet most days I am bombarded by little capsules of guilt, moments that explode and spread over me like a net. I must find some way to get away from the compulsion. It is so hard to think when it's on me, let alone write. I knew this kind of ambition afflicted other people at Yale, but it hadn't affected me until now.*

The whole elite predicament, it should be said, is not confined to the United States. The system is global and in many ways, at this point, interconnected. About a tenth of students at America's most prestigious colleges come from overseas today. Our admissions standards have diffused across the world; kids in Shanghai, Seoul, and Mumbai now are jumping through our hoops. I have heard from people in Canada, the United Kingdom, and especially South and East Asia: India, Singapore, China, South Korea, the Philippines, Japan. "I wanted to thank you for writing the most perfect, damning indictment of modern education," said one correspondent. "I'm at medical school here in Canada and your sentiments apply beyond the Ivy League." "We have our own Ivy League in India," said another. "We call them Indian Institutes of Technology (IIT) and Indian Institutes of Management (IIM). Every single thing you mentioned I have witnessed happening in practice."

Unaddressed, these issues ultimately lead to the kind of midlife crisis that is typical of high achievers. William R. Fitzsimmons, Harvard's longtime dean of admissions, has put it this way:

*It is common to encounter even the most successful students, who have won all the "prizes," stepping back and wondering if it was all worth it. Professionals in their thirties and forties— physicians, lawyers, academics, business people and others— sometimes give the impression that they are dazed survivors of some bewildering life-long boot camp. Some say they ended up in their profession because of someone else's expectations, or that they simply drifted into it without pausing to think whether they really loved their work. Often they say they missed their youth entirely, never living in the present, always pursuing some ill-defined goal.*

What then, finally, is it all for? Our glittering system of elite higher education: students kill themselves getting into it, parents kill themselves to pay for it, and always for the opportunities it opens up. But what of all the opportunities it closes down—not for any practical reason, but just because of how it smothers you with expectations? How can I become a teacher, or a minister, or a carpenter? Wouldn't that be a waste of my fancy education? What would my parents think? What would my friends think? How would I face my classmates at our twentieth reunion, when they're all rich doctors or important people in New York? And the question that exists behind them all: isn't it beneath me? So an entire world of possibilities shuts, and you miss your true calling.

That is, if you even have an inkling what your calling is. "You cannot say to a Yalie 'find your passion.' Most of us do not know how." It is indeed reasonable to say, as many students have, that you might as well go to Wall Street and make a lot of money if you can't think of anything better to do. What is not reasonable is that we have constructed an educational system that produces highly intelligent, accomplished twenty-two-year-olds who have no idea what they want to do with their lives: no sense of purpose and, what is worse, no understanding of how to go about finding one. Who can follow an existing path but don't have the imagination—or the courage, or the inner freedom—to invent their own.

# Two

## The History

How did we get here? How did the college admissions process, the fulcrum on which the system turns—casting its shadow back over childhood and adolescence and forward over college and career, shaping the way that kids are raised and thus the people they become— how did it assume its present form? It is not a phenomenon of the last ten or fifteen years. The difference between today's elite students and those of twenty or forty years ago, despite what many like to think, is only one of degree. If we want to understand where the system comes from—which means, where *we* come from, because at this point most of the American professional class has gone through it, most of its upper middle class, most of its leadership class, the people who direct our government, our economy, our culture, and our institutions— then we need to go back to the start.

In fact, we need to go back before the start, to the Gilded Age, the last decades of the nineteenth century. Contrary to popular belief, the Ivy League colleges were not always the rich-boys' finishing schools they later became. Before the Civil War, they were relatively small, relatively local institutions. The few young men who went were certainly gentlemen's sons, and gentlemen-in-training themselves, but a lot of rich boys didn't bother, and besides, in a largely agricultural society that was still fragmented into regional economies, there weren't that many rich boys to begin with.

After the war, as E. Digby Baltzell tells the story in his classic study, *The Protestant Establishment,* things began to change. Industrialization exploded, creating new fortunes and a new plutocracy. The railroad knitted the country into a single economy. The old regional elites became aware of themselves as a national elite and began to take steps to reinforce their class identity. New money needed to be socialized into gentility; all money needed to defend its social boundaries against the great unwashed, many of them Catholics and Jews, who were flooding the cities from Southern and Eastern Europe. Anti-Semitism and anti-Catholicism took hold in the upper class. The caste that Baltzell would eventually make famous as the WASPs, white Anglo-Saxon Protestants—another phenomenon we regard as eternal, but that dates, in fact, from this time—began to crystallize. "Anglo-Saxon" was very much part of the point: the English aristocracy, which the nation had rebelled against a century earlier in the name of equality, became the model for a new, American aristocracy.

The WASPs created a whole range of institutions for themselves. Exclusive resorts like Bar Harbor and Newport were up and running by 1880. The first country club was founded in 1882. Groton, not the first New England prep school but the first to be established in emulation of the venerable English public (that is, private) schools, opened its doors in 1884. *The Social Register* began publication in 1887. The Daughters of the American Revolution was founded in

1890. Soon the aristocracy was fleeing the cities for new suburban enclaves like the Philadelphia Main Line. The country day school movement followed.

One institution the WASP aristocracy did not create but did transform. Now was the time when Harvard, Yale, and Princeton assumed the moneyed shape of legend: the Harvard of the "Gold Coast" of private dormitories; the Yale of *Stover at Yale,* a famous campus novel of the time; the Princeton of F. Scott Fitzgerald (which gentrified its name from the College of New Jersey in 1896). Elite colleges, where affluent young men could mingle with their peers from across the country, played a crucial role in inculcating mores, establishing connections, and certifying graduates as members of the leadership class. As colleges sought to entice a new kind of customer by dispelling their bookish image, extracurriculars— especially athletics, and most especially the "manly" sport of football, which was invented in its current form at elite schools at exactly this time—began to play a central role in campus life. Business boomed; Harvard expanded from 100 students a year in the 1860s to more than 600 by 1904. Academics were out—something only "drips" or "grinds" would bother with. Parties, pranks, and snobbery were in, as social life was taken over by the prep school crowd, which came to dominate numerically, as well. The Big Three, as they were baptized in the 1880s, became "iconic institutions," in the words of Jerome Karabel, setting the fashion for campuses across the country.

But soon there was a problem, as Karabel explains in *The Chosen: The Hidden History of Admission and Exclusion at Harvard, Yale, and Princeton.* Admissions were based on entrance exams. On the one hand, kids from feeder schools would often be let in no matter how badly they did. (Of the 405 Grotonians who applied to Harvard from 1906 to 1932, the school rejected three.) On the other hand, because the subjects covered, particularly Greek and Latin, were not available in public schools, the majority of high school graduates—and back then, there weren't that many to begin with—were automatically excluded. The social tone was preserved, but academic standards plummeted. By 1916, all three colleges had dropped their classical language requirements. Enrollment from public high schools soared—but public high schools, especially in the big cities, were increasingly populated by Jews. Columbia, the cautionary example, cut its proportion of Jews almost in half, from 40 percent, in two years, but not before experiencing a permanent exodus of upper-class families.

The Big Three were not going to let that happen to them. A whole new set of admissions criteria was developed to hold back the Semitic tide by making sure that the "right sort" of student got in: letters of recommendation, alumni interviews, the preference for athletes and "leaders," special treatment for sons of alumni (that is, "legacies"), an emphasis on geographic distribution, and a devaluation of pure academic ability. Better midwestern Protestants, even if they weren't all the sharpest tools in the shed, than "greasy grinds" from Brooklyn. Princeton started requiring applicants to submit a photo, since you couldn't always tell from the name. "Character" became the explicit ideal: manners, looks, tone, being a "Yale man"—all once guaranteed by where you went to school, now enforced through a subjective process of evaluation (and the admissions offices that had to be created to conduct it).

The system endured, largely intact, until the 1960s. The Big Three continued to be dominated by prep school graduates; most of their students still came from wealthy families; unofficial quotas kept the Jewish numbers down; the old-boy, handshake, feeder-school culture remained in place. As late as 1950, Harvard received only thirteen applications for every ten spots, while Yale's acceptance rate was 46 percent. You knew if you were welcome, and if you weren't you didn't bother to apply.

But already by the 1930s, forces had started to gather that would eventually destroy the old way of doing things. James B. Conant, newly installed as president of Harvard, began to take steps to raise academic standards, increase access, and tap the nation's talent pool. To identify the bright young men who would, to be sure, only supplement the school's existing clientele, he turned to a recently developed "psychometric" test: the SAT. Conant was a reformer, not a revolutionary. Change was incremental over the next three decades. The average SAT score at elite colleges before World War II was around 500, right in the middle of the distribution; by the early 1960s, it had risen to about 625.

The revolution came at Yale that decade under Kingman Brewster. Like Conant, Brewster recognized that if the American elite was going to retain its position (and the country it led, its preeminence), it would have to make itself accessible to rising social groups—and that, if for no other reason than their own self-interest, the colleges that trained that elite would have to take the lead. Changes were happening in American life that the Big Three could no longer ignore. Within a couple of years of assuming the presidency of the university in 1963, Brewster had elevated academic promise to supremacy among admissions criteria, shunted aside the ideal of the well-rounded man in favor of the "brilliant specialist," reduced the preferences for athletes and legacies, eliminated the checklist of physical characteristics that had played a role in the admissions process (resulting in a drop of nearly half an inch in the average height of the incoming class), ended the college's cozy relationship with its feeder schools, removed the Jewish quota, and instituted need-blind admissions. Affirmative action was introduced by the last years of the decade. In 1969, the school became coed.

Brewster had demolished the old system at a single blow. The school's alumni forced him to reverse a few of his reforms, particularly those concerning athletes and legacies, but the point of no return had been passed. Nineteen sixty-five, the year of Brewster's revolution—which was also right around the time the baby boomers started to arrive on campus—can be taken as the pivot, in college admissions, from the old aristocracy to the new meritocracy: from caste, "character," and connections to scores and grades.

**And that is the origin** of the system that we are still living with today. Yet things are not as different from the old procedure as they seem. Never mind the preferences for athletes, legacies, and others. Brewster, and everyone around the country who followed his lead, expanded access on a monumental scale, but they didn't really discard the old criteria, for the most part; they simply supplemented them. We don't ask applicants to do something different now; we ask them to do almost everything they used to have to do, plus a whole lot more.

Think of what we want from kids today, if they're going to be admitted to an elite college. We want them to be, not athletes exactly, not performers at the highest level, but sportsmen, in the old term, people with a certain skill and grace—a demand they satisfy, in some cases, by playing games that derive from the prep school tradition (fencing, crew) and that exist nowhere else in American life. We want them to develop a measure of artistic ability, to engage in the kind of idiosyncratic self-cultivation that was a hallmark of the upper-class ideal, with its resources of leisure and culture. We want them to be personable—or as people used to call it, clubbable—so we still require an interview and letters of recommendation. We want them to demonstrate a commitment to "service," which is nothing other than a modern echo of noblesse oblige, and generally under-taken in the same spirit of benign condescension. And we want them to be "leaders." It's not enough to participate in student government, say; you have to run it. You have to be president of the theater club, or captain of the baseball team. You have to come across, in other words, as an oligarch in training, just like the private school boys of a century ago.

But to all this now, to an admissions process that was designed to select for an upper-class profile, we have added Brewster's re-quirements for academic excellence—which, as we saw, was decid-edly not a part of the upper-class profile. Now we have the whole regime of SAT, AP, GPA, National Merit, and so forth. Now our kids must have the qualities of both an old aristocrat and a modern tech-nocrat. No wonder they're so busy, and so frantic.

The only thing that's changed since the mid-1960s is that every-thing has gotten inexorably worse: the admissions rates lower, the expectations higher, the competition fiercer, the pressure on stu-dents greater. Once the starting gun of meritocracy was fired, it was everybody off to the races. Already by 1968, acceptance rates at Har-vard, Yale, and Princeton had fallen to around 20 percent. By 1974, according to Nicholas Lemann in *The Big Test,* "a whole culture of obsession" with SAT scores had developed in American high schools (a fact that I remember well from the talk of my older siblings, who were going through the system at exactly this time). The expansion of the college-age cohort in the 1970s intensified the pressure, as did the number of students actually finishing their degrees, since the more BAs were out there, the more imperative it was felt to be to distinguish yourself by going to a big-name school.

By the end of the decade, Lemann says, affluent families had started to game the system with SAT tutors, application-essay "ad-visors" (that is, ghostwriters), strategic alumni donations, and other tactics. Colleges were letting it be known that they wanted to see as many Advanced Placement courses as possible on high school transcripts—and if you were going to be ready for APs by junior or senior year, you had to start accelerating as early as middle school. As the baby boom passed out of the system in the early 1980s, colleges began to recruit prospective applicants more intensively. The deregulation of the airline and telecommunications industries helped make the higher education market fully national, since now it was cheaper to send your child across the country and to stay in touch once she was there. Early admissions programs, which lock kids into specific schools, grew ever more important as a way for colleges to gain an edge against their rivals.

Then came the earthquake: *U.S. News & World Report*, a weak third among American newsweeklies, debuted its college rankings in 1983. Admissions statistics had long been regarded as a measure of institutional prestige, but now there was a single set of figures that encompassed every college in the country, a single number that defined the status of a school. Already in 1987, a delegation of college presidents asked the magazine to stop, but it was too late, because it was too profitable. Now the madness shifted to a higher gear. The decade saw the explosion of the college admissions industry: test prep, tutors, guidebooks, consultants. The writer Caitlin Flanagan mentions a book called *How to Get Into an Ivy League School* (1985), among the first of its kind. According to Tom Wolfe, "the pandemic known as college mania" began "to show its true virulence" in 1988.

The point is not which date is right. They're all right. Pick any moment over the last half century and things will be worse afterward than they were before. In the last couple of decades, the admissions pool has gone from national to global. The decline in the college-age population reversed itself in 1997, reaching boomer levels once again within a decade. Schools are ever more adept at juking their admissions stats, using aggressive marketing practices to gin up larger and larger numbers of applicants, many of whom they know they'll never admit (the so-called "attract to reject" strategy), just to lower their acceptance rates. Nor is it only a matter of status; schools, like other businesses, borrow money, and credit rating agencies take admissions statistics into account. No less than corporate profits, the numbers are expected to get better every year.

Perhaps most crucial, in creating the feeling that the last couple of decades represent something new, is the fact that we're into the second generation now. The parents of the kids who have been going through the system since the early 1990s are products, increasingly, of the system themselves. People who sent their children to elite colleges in the 1970s and '80s were much more likely to have gone to less prestigious, often public universities, or not to have gone to college at all. Now we're dealing with a cohort of meritocratic professionals for whom a different sort of life is inconceivable. What was once an opportunity has become a necessity. There is only one definition of happiness, and only one way to get it.

Since 1992, admissions rates have fallen by more than a third at 17 of the top 20 liberal arts colleges in the current *U.S. News* ranking, and by more than half at 18 of the top 20 universities. They have fallen from 65 percent to 14 percent at Vanderbilt, from 45 percent to 13 percent at the University of Chicago, and from 32 percent to 7 percent at Columbia. Early applications rose at Duke by 23 percent in 2011 alone, on top of a 14 percent increase the previous year. In 2013, Harvard, Stanford, and Columbia, which each admit fewer than 2,500 students, all received more than 31,000 applications, over 50 percent more than they had only six years earlier.

●   ●   ●

**If those of us who** went to college in the 1970s and '80s no longer recognize the admissions process, if today's elite students appear to be an alien species—Super People, perhaps, or a race of bionic hamsters—that is only because the logic of the system that was put in place in the 1960s, when the genteel bigotry of the old boys' network gave way to an egalitarian war of all against all, has been playing out for that much longer. When I graduated from high school in 1981, the kids who got into the most prestigious colleges took about three AP courses and did about three extracurricular activities each. Now the numbers are more apt to be seven or eight of the former and nine or ten of the latter. When I sat on the Yale admissions committee in 2008 (faculty members rotate through for a single day), kids who had five or six items on their list of extracurriculars—the so-called "brag" in admissions lingo, it was the first thing the officer would mention when presenting a case—were already in trouble, because that wasn't nearly enough. In *Privilege*, Ross Douthat refers to a fellow student who had twelve, "a typically jam-packed Harvard résumé." I once had a freshman advisee who had done eleven APs.

None of this, I should say, is the fault of the admissions offices, which are acting on instructions from on high. During my day on the committee, I was deeply impressed by the staff. Admissions officers not only plow through thousands of folders during the long winter months; they are intimately conversant with the geographic areas for which they are responsible. We were doing eastern Pennsylvania that day in my subcommittee—suburban Philadelphia, essentially—and the junior officer in charge (it was only one of his regions), a young man who looked to be about thirty, was familiar, to a remarkable level of detail, not only with the high schools and the guidance counselors, with whom he had developed relationships over countless recruiting trips, but also with the alumni interviewers and outside readers who assisted with the territory.

It was spring; early admissions had already been done. Applicants, each represented by a long string of figures and codes (SATs, GPA, class rank, numerical scores to which the letters of recommendation had been converted, special notations for athletes, legacies, diversity cases, and so forth), had been assigned a single cumulative score from 1 to 4. The 1's had already been admitted; when I asked to see an example during the lunch break, I was shown the winner of the Intel Science Talent Search, formerly known as the Westinghouse. Threes and 4's, which made up about three-quarters of the remainder, could get in only under special conditions: a nationally ranked athlete or a "DevA," an applicant in the highest category of "development" cases (that is, children of very rich donors, who get admitted under almost any circumstances). Now we were adjudicating, for the most part, among the 2's. In six hours of committee work, we disposed of somewhere between 100 and 125 cases, or about three or four minutes per applicant, looking for 10–15 admissions to fill out the rough allotment of approximately 40 for the region.

The junior officer presented each case, rat-a-tat-tat, in a blizzard of admissions jargon that I had to pick up on the fly. "Top checks": the top boxes had been checked in every category on the letters. "Good rig": the transcript exhibits a good degree of academic rigor. "Ed level 1": parents have an educational level no higher than high school, indicating a genuine hardship case. "Lacrosse #3": third on the coach's wish list. "MUSD": a musician in the highest category of promise ("Distinguished"), indicating a potential professional career. "T1": first letter; "E1": first essay; "TX": extra letter; "SR": guidance counselor. We listened, asked questions, dove into a letter or two, then voted up or down ("we" meaning three admissions staff altogether, a member of the college dean's office, and me, who mainly deferred to the pros). Huge bowls of junk food were stationed at the side of the room to keep our energy up. The dean of admissions—who looked like Ben Stein, and who could really spin an application folder—seemed to subsist on a diet of Doritos.

With so many accomplished applicants to choose from, we were looking for kids with something special, "PQs"—personal qualities—that were often revealed by the letters or essays. Kids who only had the numbers and the resume were usually rejected: "no spark," "not a team-builder," "this is pretty much in the middle of the fairway for us." One young man who had piled up a truly insane quantity of extracurriculars, and who submitted eight letters of recommendation, was felt to be "too intense." On the other hand, the numbers and the resume were clearly indispensable. I'd been told in the orientation that morning that successful applicants could either be "well-rounded" or "pointy"—outstanding in one particular way—but if they were pointy, they had to be *really* pointy: a musician whose audition tape had impressed the music department, a scientist who had won a national award.

So almost everybody had to be well-rounded, but that means something very different now than it did in the days of Dink Stover. The older ideal, the prep school boy, was indeed displaced by Brewster's brilliant specialists. Now the colleges talk about assembling a well-rounded *class* by bringing together a variety of "well-lopsided" students: a junior journalist, a budding astronomer, a future diplomat, a language whiz. Those ten extracurricular activities that a typical admitted student has will not all go in ten different directions. Three or four or five will represent a special area of focus: math or art or student government. You have to be great at one or two things—but you also have to be really, really good at everything else: "well" as well as "lopsided." You may already know that you aren't going to be a scientist or anything else that involves advanced mathematics, but you still have to sign up for calculus ("good rig"), and you still have to ace it (class rank, GPA). You might be one of those "passionate weirdos" who'd rather spend his time writing poetry or computer code, but you have to play your instruments and do your sports and join (or better yet, start) your clubs and rush around from thing to thing. You have, in other words, to do it all: get A's in all your classes, compete for leadership positions, pile up the extracurriculars—be a Super Person.

**That is why the college** admissions process—and the people it produces—have become unrecognizable in recent years. External factors like globalization and even *U.S. News* are only the smaller part of the story. The main thing that's driving the madness is simply the madness itself. "The resume arms race," as it is invariably called, is just like the nuclear one. The only point of having more is having more than everybody else. Nobody needed 20,000 atomic warheads until the other side had 19,000. Nobody needs eleven extracurriculars, either—what purpose does having them actually serve?—unless the other guy has ten. So like giraffes evolving ever-longer necks, our kids keep getting more and more deformed. Just what they're going to look like in another twenty years is anybody's guess.

The system, it should be said, goes well beyond the most prestigious schools: the HYPSters (Harvard, Yale, Princeton, and Stanford); or the eight members of the Ivy League; or the Golden Dozen, as Andrew Hacker and Claudia Dreifus refer to them in *Higher Education?*, the Ivies plus Stanford, Duke, Williams, and Amherst. The greatest extremes—the fattest resumes and the most anorexic acceptance rates—will always be found at the same few schools, but as my travels and conversations over the last few years have shown me, the mania exists, albeit at lower temperatures, at a much larger pool of institutions. The students I met at the University of Virginia may not have had nine or ten extracurriculars on their resume, but they did have six or seven. The ones I talked with at the Honors College of the University of Mississippi may not have done seven or eight APs, but they did do five or six. The logic and the values are the same across a wide array of schools, even if the level of ambition, or aptitude, or neurosis, or parental wealth is not.

It's one big system, after all. Those thirty-three thousand students who are now turned away from Harvard each year go somewhere else. As of 2012, sixty-five colleges and universities could boast acceptance rates of 33 percent or less. Add another two or three dozen places that are close to the line, or whose rates are higher for one reason or another (women's colleges, for instance, which necessarily draw from a smaller pool), and there are maybe a hundred schools that can plausibly be said to belong to the elite. But even that underestimates the size of the phenomenon. I have heard from people at a variety of regional liberal arts colleges—schools that are not "names" in any sense, but that enroll a lot of bright and ambitious students—and they have told me that the issues are the same there, too. James Fallows estimates that about 10–15 percent of high school graduates are caught up in the competition for spots at selective schools. That amounts to something like four hundred thousand kids a year. It is to the kind of childhoods those kids endure—the parents, the high schools, the inner life of excellent sheep—that I turn in the following chapter.

# Three

## The Training

Families are scared, and for good reason. Social mobility has stalled. The global playing field is getting ever more competitive. The middle class is hanging on by its fingernails, and the upper middle class seems harder than ever to reach. The future, since 2008, has looked more daunting, especially for young people, than at any other time in memory. A college degree, we hear incessantly, is absolutely indispensable, and—though this is more dubious—the more prestigious the college the better. If you live in a winner-take-all society, you're going to want your child to be among the winners.

But let's not kid ourselves. The admissions frenzy has been raging, in good times and bad, for close to fifty years, not six. It is not primarily about the lower and middle classes seeking to rise, or even about the upper middle class attempting to maintain its position. It is about determining the exact hierarchy of status within the upper middle class itself. Fallows's 10–15 percent, the share of high school students who participate in the selective admissions process, may not correspond precisely to the upper 10–15 percent of the income distribution (there is still a certain proportion of strivers who manage to get through the door, especially from immigrant communities), but it does correspond pretty closely. In 2012, the top 15 percent of household incomes began at $117,000.

The college admissions game, in the affluent suburbs and well-heeled urban enclaves where it is principally played, is not about whether you go to an elite school. It's about which one you go to. It is Penn versus Tufts, not Penn versus Penn State. It doesn't matter that a bright young person can still go to Ohio State, become a doctor, settle in Bloomington or Dayton, and make a very good living. Such an outcome is simply too horrible to contemplate. Hence, in the words of a mother who wrote me, "this aggressive suburban wasting disease, this high-achievement addiction." "The pressure out here is ridiculous," another mother, from a Boston suburb, told me. "It is obscene."

While the overbearing upper-middle-class parent is a familiar figure now, there is a contradiction in the usual account. We all know about the helicopter parent—hovering, pressuring, criticizing—and about the kind of structured, supervised, skill-building childhood they superintend. The governing word is "let's," as in, "Let's practice your piano now." We also know about the overindulgent parent—the kind who lets their kids run wild in restaurants, who's still tying their shoelaces on their eighth birthday, who constantly tells them what wonderful, unique snowflakes they are, how they can be anything they want when they grow up, how they should do what they love and follow their dreams.

The two parental styles are not, however, antithetical. They spring from a common impulse. Coddling and pushing, stroking and surveillance, are both forms of overprotection. Each bespeaks a misguided belief that you can make the world safe for your children: that if you only do everything right, nothing will ever impede or harm them—that you can shield them, in the words of Peggy Orenstein, "from pain or failure or sadness." Helicopter parenting, as Anna Quindlen has said, originates in the illusion of control. One might add that it is a particularly middle-class form of that illusion: the idea that life can be rendered predictable, reduced to an orderly succession of achievements that will guarantee security and comfort. Pressuring your kids to get an A in calculus when they are seventeen is essentially the same as tying their shoelaces for them when they are eight. Both are ways of treating them as if they can't do anything for themselves.

Both, in other words, are forms of infantilization. "They have not grown up," writes Harry R. Lewis of the students he knew as dean of Harvard College, "and that is the way everyone seems to want it." ("From a psychoanalytic or therapeutic point of view," a former student wrote me, "the alliance that the university forms with parents is never benign, and for a lot of students at elite schools it can be monstrous.") It should not surprise us that so many kids move home after college—another trend that started long before the financial collapse. The only question is, how many of their parents are secretly glad when it happens? "We were going to do the right thing and raise perfect kids," a father said to me, conflating in one word these two contradictory impulses: "perfect" as in perfectly happy, "perfect" as in perfectly accomplished. As for why you'd feel the need to raise such paragons, or believe that it is possible, or think that trying to do so is desirable, perhaps the answer is that the only lovable children are "perfect" ones.

Both kinds of parenting, finally, are forms of overidentification. The helicopter parent turns the child into an instrument of her will. The overindulgent parent projects his own need for limitless freedom and security. In either case, the child is made to function as an extension of somebody else. This is the essential fact of high-achievement parenting today. In *The Price of Privilege*, the clinical psychologist Madeline Levine speaks of parents "who fill up their own brittle selves with their children's accomplishments." In *The Pale King*, David Foster Wallace has his narrator remark that "it was a little bit like a for-profit company, my family, in that you were pretty much only as good as your last sales quarter." (An acute observer of the elite mentality, Wallace writes elsewhere of the difference between feeling "val*ued*," as a child, and feeling "valu*able*.") In the words of Michael G. Thompson, the author of many books on personality development, "The delegating family sends a child out, and the child believes that she is free and independent, but in fact she is on a mission for her parents that must be fulfilled."

Many pressures converge here: status competition within extended families; peer pressure within communities; the desire to measure up to your own parents, or to best them; "family branding," as somebody put it to me. When your kid gets into a prestigious college, it's as if you got an A in being a parent. And nothing less than that, of course, will do.

Nor is college the end of it, needless to say. "My office," Levine writes, "has seen an endless stream of bright, talented children who are disinterested in school because 'My parents think there are only two things to be in the world: a doctor or a lawyer.'" A Stanford student told me that his parents let him know that if he switched from engineering to humanities, they'd cease to pay his tuition. A recent Yale graduate who is pursuing a teaching career despite parental opposition wrote about "a mother bent on 'opening doors for me' and pushing me into an elite that she eyed with desire from the middle class. She wanted me to have everything instead of wanting me to have what I wanted."

But what about "do what you love" and "follow your dreams"? Well, that's just the thing. Parents may say that sort of stuff, and they may sincerely believe that they mean it, but no one else is fooled. The schools aren't fooled. An administrator at a private high school told me that parents say that they like the idea that their kids are being taught to be creative and independent thinkers, but when crunch time comes, what they care about is the prestige admissions. "I'm not the kind of parent who calls all the time," another administrator told me, is what every parent starts with when they call.

More important, the kids aren't fooled. In *"Doing School": How We Are Creating a Generation of Stressed Out, Materialistic, and Miseducated Students,* Denise Clark Pope quotes one hyperanxious high school junior who is running a 3.97 GPA: "They are worried about me and say that it's okay if I don't go to an Ivy school, like they'll still be proud of me, but that's b.s. because no they won't." Levine puts it like this:

> *I understand the contempt of my teenage patients who roll their eyes in session when a parent says, "Your grades aren't good enough, we know you can do better," or the ubiquitous "Just do your best." Too often these duplicitous statements are used to mask a disturbing truth, that what is expected by many parents in affluent communities is not a personal best but the absolute best.*

Parents of high achievers are often oblivious, even willfully so, to what their kids are going through. Levine cites a raft of troubling statistics: "Preteens and teens from affluent, well-educated families . . . experience among the highest rates of depression, substance abuse, anxiety disorders, somatic complaints, and unhappiness of any group of children in this country." "As many as 22 percent of adolescent girls from financially comfortable families suffer from clinical depression." Mental health problems "can be two to five times more prevalent among private high school juniors and seniors" than among their public school counterparts. When problems occur, she says, affluent parents are also less likely to acknowledge them, in part because academic success is seen as a sign of maturity and emotional health.

Perhaps most disturbing of all, affluent teenagers feel less connected to their parents than do any other group of teens, including poor ones. Praise, Levine says, is not warmth, and the vaunted self-esteem that parents are so keen to instill is not the same as self-efficacy, the belief in your ability to get things done in the world. Hovering and criticism, adds William Damon, author of *The Path to Purpose* and many other books on child development, should not be confused with attention or guidance. High-pressure parents, as one of Levine's young patients puts it, are "everywhere and nowhere at the same time." They are intrusive, but they are not connected.

**Fortunately, one of those parents** has blessed us with a perfect portrait of the type, Amy Chua's *Battle Hymn of the Tiger Mother*. A lot of people denounced the book when it was published in 2011; a lot of people celebrated it, as its author intended we should, as a rebuke to our lazy American parenting style. Of course, it is nothing of the sort. Chua's "Asian" parenting is simply an extreme version of upper-middle-class practice—the unrelenting pressure as she hounds her daughters to excel, the willful disregard of everything except "achievement"—and it shows us all that's wrong with it and all that lies behind it. Perusing her book is like reading a novel with an unreliable narrator: she is constantly revealing things she doesn't realize about herself, is blind to the meaning of her own story.

Chua champions filial obedience, but the father she reveres rebelled against his own parents, and she rebelled against him in turn: he by leaving China for the United States, she by leaving California for the East Coast. (Both, it seems, were trying to get as far away as possible.) By her own admission, she made a long series of mistakes about her career, and for all the predictable reasons: trying to please her family, following the path of least resistance, not acknowledging her true desires. She holds up her mother-in-law as the archetypal example of the bad American parent—someone who believes in wishy-washy concepts like choice, independence, creativity, and the importance of questioning authority—yet this is a woman who produced a son whom Chua herself found worthy of marriage and who turned out to be successful even on his wife's own terms: accepted at Princeton, then Juilliard, then Harvard Law, a professor at Yale and a bestselling author to boot.

But all of this is lost on her when it comes to raising her children. The needs that drive her reign of terror (the term is not too strong) are a compound of panicked perfectionism and an infantile sense of entitlement. Amid her reams of artless boasting—about herself, her kids, her husband, her sisters—the salient terms are "greatest," "famous," "said to be surpassed . . . only by," and so forth: status-mongering at its most unreflective. There is no middle ground; Chua's psyche seems to balance on a knife edge between glory and abjection. If you're not the best, you're a "loser." If you're not brilliant, you're worthless. It is altogether to the point that the book's most famous scene, the one where Chua rejects her daughters' birthday cards as showing insufficient evidence of effort, takes place at a "mediocre restaurant." The great Amy Chua deserves a nicer set of birthday cards, just as she deserves something better than "stale focaccia."

No wonder she is willing to do whatever it takes to make sure that her daughters don't turn out to be "losers," too, fit only to be cast aside like stale focaccia, even if it means destroying their happiness. Neither one of them has friends, she tells us (or others tell her, at least, since she cannot seem to take the information in). Well, she says, "The truth is I'm not good at enjoying life"—so why then, is the implication, should her daughters be? Happiness is not the point; the point is control. "In Chinese thinking," she explains, "the child is the extension of the self." Parental narcissism does not get more explicit than that. But Chua does not finally seem like a parent at all. Still an extension of her own parents—forever feeling their eyes upon her, incapable of questioning the values with which she was raised—she remains an eternal child, insatiable in her demands for love and attention. As for her own children, the fact that one has gotten into Harvard now is not a validation of her methods. It is a condemnation of Harvard's, and of the system as a whole. Of course her daughter got into Harvard: that is exactly the kind of parenting the system rewards. That's exactly what is wrong with it.

My sense, as I have spoken with teachers at elite high schools, is that most understand what is wrong and wish they could do better by their students. Teachers at exclusive schools, one told me, are often "excellent black sheep"—people who were raised that way themselves, accumulated their share of accolades, then decided there was something more to life. Some have described the ways they try to smuggle different values into the classroom, like love of learning or service to the community. The problem is they don't have any room to operate. One teacher at a prep school in Westchester told me of a student breaking down in tears during a discussion of *Catcher in the Rye*. He didn't want to have to be a stockbroker, like his parents said. That very night, she got a call from the boy's mother: "Don't put any ideas into his head."

Some localities have tried to take the pressure down. Ridgewood,

New Jersey, an upscale suburb, has instituted a voluntary day off from homework and extracurricular activities, and other communities have followed suit. But it tells us everything we need to know about the state of things that the program involves taking off, not one day a week, but one day a year. But even that's too much for many people. A teacher at a private school has told me of parents refusing to allow their children to go on a field trip, because they couldn't afford to lose a day of academics—and of a lot of kids agreeing with them.

It doesn't matter if your parents aren't crazy, I've been told again and again, because the environment is. Other people's parents are crazy, so the whole school is crazy. And however well-intentioned teachers often are, principals and other supervisors tend to work against them. Teachers are trapped in the system, as well, as one of them told me. A veteran of many years, she has watched her institution evolve in the direction of a customer-service mentality: give the parents what they want, no matter what's good for the kids. Don't challenge them intellectually, don't encourage them to engage the material, don't even try to insist on academic rigor.

That may be the most damning thing about these schools, so full of smart teachers teaching the smart children of smart parents: that they finally don't care about learning at all. "Don't put any ideas into his head": a request that is honored all too well. Everybody wants their child to get an education, but nobody wants them to get an *education* education. A series that was published in a Palo Alto paper—Palo Alto, of all places—portrays an environment at the local high schools that is "hostile to learning." The kids in *"Doing School"* rarely hear that education might be valuable for its own sake. "I went to Hopkins, a Yale feeder school, and *hated* it," a former student wrote me. "The place turned learning into a simple endurance test, blithely awarding the best 'athletes.'"

The whole of childhood and adolescence, across a large swath of society, is now constructed with a single goal in mind. All the values that once informed the way we raise our children—the cultivation of curiosity, the inculcation of character, the instillment of a sense of membership in one's community, the development of the capacity for democratic citizenship, let alone any emphasis on the pleasure and freedom of play, the part of childhood where you actually get to be a child—all these are gone. As the sociologist Mitchell L. Stevens has put it, "affluent families fashion an entire way of life organized around the production of measurable virtue in children." Measurable, here, means capable of showing up on a college application. We are not teaching to the test; we're living to it.

**What can such a circumstance** produce, if not the full demonology of psychological suffering? One of my students compared the situation to women's gymnastics. Think of the mood that prevails on the competition floor every four years at the Olympics, tense with a kind of anorexic perfectionism: no margin for error, no joy in the work, no room to hide from scrutiny, success understood as the absence of failure. Levine writes of teens feeling "pressured, misunderstood, anxious, angry, sad, and empty"—in short, "dreadfully unhappy"—and of responding with eating disorders, cutting, substance abuse, addiction, depression, antisocial behavior, and suicidal thoughts.

Eve, the girl who's running a 3.97 in *"Doing School"*—she is carrying four APs her junior year, plans to do seven her senior year, and copes with the workload, among other ways, by studying in class (that is, for other classes)—has this to say: "I sometimes have two or three days where I only get two hours of sleep per night. . . . I really really fear failure. . . . I am just a machine with no life at this place. . . . I am a robot just going page by page, doing the work." She "surviv[es] on cereal" but is usually "too stressed and tired to feel hungry"—though not so stressed that, like some of her friends, she talks about killing herself. And yet she wouldn't have it any other way: "Some people see health and happiness as more important than grades and college; I don't."

Levine speaks of addiction in the usual respect, but the mechanics of addiction operate for high-achieving students in a wider sense, as well. Addicts often say the reason that they need a fix is that it makes them feel, not good, exactly, but "all right." The drug no longer gives them pleasure; it only takes away the pain—the pain, that is, of needing the drug. So it is with the drug of praise upon which these children are trained to depend: the praise that is the sign of parental love, for the achievement that is the condition of that love. Every A is a fix that temporarily quells the anxiety of failure, the terror of falling short.

This is all that famous "self-esteem," the quality that parents are so keen to instill, amounts to. It is a balloon that must be kept perpetually inflated by the hot air of approval ("val*ued*," not "valu*able*"), and it collapses at the first contact with reality. Levine writes of young people who have no ability to handle setbacks, like the girl who contemplates suicide because her SAT scores are a little lower than she expected, or the boy who, cut from the basketball team, is terrified of going home to face his father's disappointment. Hence the reason the admissions process often proves to be so devastating. For the first time in their lives, a lot of kids who are used to nothing but success are forced to deal with failure. One of my students remarked that the movie *Black Swan,* about a ballerina who goes through a psychotic break, reminded her of a lot of her peers: so perfectionistic that they no longer live in reality. Perfectionism, Levine explains, is a desperate attempt to stave off criticism—which, as practiced in ambitious households, is not the disapproval of a child's actions, but the condemnation of her very self. It is the inverse of praise; it fosters self-hatred by telling the child that he isn't worthy of his parents' love.

**And here we come to** the heart of the matter, as Alice Miller laid it out in her classic psychoanalytic study, *The Drama of the Gifted Child*. In Miller's account, the self of the "gifted" or accomplished child is formed in response to the parents' need for gratification through achievement (typically rooted in their own "brittle selves," as Levine reminds us, the result of the same kind of upbringing). The child gives his parents what he understands they want, becomes the person that they need him to be. But the demand is insatiable, because its satisfaction is always provisional. The child is "never good enough" ("only as good as your last sales quarter"), and so he tries to be perfect. Once this expectation is internalized, of course, it doesn't matter where the needed affirmation comes from. All achievement becomes a stand-in for parental approval. "He seeks insatiably for admiration," Miller writes, "of which he never gets enough because admiration is not the same thing as love."

And so, Miller says, the gifted child—no longer necessarily a child, needless to say—swings incessantly between the poles of grandiosity and depression. Grandiosity is the delusion of supremacy. It's what your parents told you when you *did* live up to their expectations: You're perfect! You're the best! You can do anything you want! It is self-esteem at its most distended, that rush you get when you ace your SATs or get the job at Goldman. The internal monologue goes something like this: "Screw you all—I win." Grandiosity is what you're in the grips of as you lay your plans for world domination, whatever that might mean for you. Depression is the state that ensues when you suffer a setback, and the delusion collapses. Depression means self-loathing, self-disgust, and the kind of emotional numbness that feels like psychic death. It also means self-punishment, which, among other things, is all those thoughts you use to make yourself feel bad—"I'm not good enough," "I'm not smart enough," "I don't work hard enough," "So-and-so is better than me," etc., etc.—and which stems from the feeling that you don't deserve to be happy. "If I didn't take Zoloft," a former student told me, "I would hate myself." Grandiosity involves contempt for others; depression involves contempt for yourself.

We had a cruder name for this dynamic, back when I was in my twenties: "hot shit/piece of shit." Either you're up or you're down, totally cool or utterly worthless. "I spent about 50% of my time at Yale feeling smug because I was smarter than everyone," a former student wrote me. "I spent the other 50% feeling shitty because everyone was smarter than me." It is this kind of thinking that lies behind the all-or-nothing mentality that one invariably finds among high achievers. To hear people talk, there is no middle ground between a mansion and the gutter, the Ivy League and total disgrace, Carnegie Hall and being, as Amy Chua would say, a loser. Philip Roth has his hero put it this way in *Portnoy's Complaint*:

> *What was it with these Jewish parents, what, that they were able to make us little Jewish boys believe ourselves to be princes on the one hand, unique as unicorns on the one hand, geniuses and brilliant like nobody has ever been brilliant and beautiful before in the history of childhood—saviors and sheer perfection on the one hand, and such bumbling, incompetent, thoughtless, helpless, selfish, evil little shits, little ingrates, on the other!*

Here we see that famous Jewish guilt, amply attested in other traditions as well: the sense of criminality that comes from failing to give your parents *naches*, pleasure—or in more familiar terms, to make them proud.

I should say that this is very personal for me. Everything I'm talking about is very personal, because I used to be one of these kids, but this above all. For years I rode the roller coaster of grandiosity and depression, struggled to separate myself from the need for my father's approval. (He was both an immigrant and an Ivy League professor, a double whammy.) Even getting a job at Yale turned out to be, like every achievement, no more than a temporary salve. Within a few months, he was asking me when I was going to get my dissertation published. But he wasn't the real problem anymore, and his death, a decade later, made very little difference. The real problem was, as one of my students has put it, "the Frankenstein's monster of ambition," the insatiable need to be "the best."

Time and again I'd thought I'd finally gotten over it, and time and again I would relapse. It was only when I read *The Drama of the Gifted Child* in the course of researching this book—I was already forty-eight, with half of my adulthood gone—that I was finally able to find relief. Actually, it was only when I read *The Drama of the Gifted Child* directly after *Battle Hymn of the Tiger Mother*. (Thank you, Amy Chua.) *Tiger Mother* felt like reliving a childhood trauma; *The Drama of the Gifted Child* felt like going through the therapy to cure it. Both show, from opposite directions but in terms that are equally stark, what it was that I'd grown up with. Something broke in me, or rather, something broke loose. I suddenly felt—not only saw, as I had for many years, but felt—that I was missing my life. I was missing my chance to be happy, missing my chance to be free.

I was also missing something else: the joy that comes when you stop feeling threatened by other people's accomplishments and let yourself be open to the beauty that they bring into the world. For that is one of the greatest curses of the high-achieving mentality: the envy that it forces on you—the desperation, not simply to be loved, but to be loved, as Auden says, alone. Milton, in *Paradise Lost*, has Satan put it like this—Satan, who is not a beastlike creature in the poem, but the brightest of the angels, the first in his class, fallen, precisely, from excess ambition. He has arrived in Eden to destroy the happiness of Adam and Eve, and looking around himself, he thinks:

> *the more I see*
> *Pleasures about me, so much more I feel*
> *Torment within me, as from the hateful siege*
> *Of contraries; all good to me becomes*
> *Bane, and in Heav'n much worse would be my state.*

That's how envy works: the better things are, the worse they are, because they don't belong to you. Or as Satan puts it more succinctly elsewhere in the poem, "myself am Hell." But now I'd finally had enough. I wasn't going to be guilty anymore. I wasn't going to punish myself by looking for reasons to be miserable. I wasn't going to feel bad about feeling good. I had spent enough time in Hell. But it had taken more than thirty years to reach that point.

**The self that forms in** response to parental expectations is, in Miller's terms, a "false self." Because the child's feelings and desires are not validated or acknowledged, she learns to ignore them and eventually loses the capacity to recognize them. Such parents, Miller writes, cannot tolerate a child who is "sad, needy, angry, furious"—a dark foreshadowing of that contemporary impulse to shield your kids, as Orenstein put it, "from pain or failure or sadness." The result is that affable, competent, adult-oriented personality that today's young high achievers are so famous for. Rather than developing an inner self with its own goals and values, they become dependent, for their sense of who they are, on authority figures and the tokens of approval they distribute. Levine's patients, she says, will often speak of themselves the way you'd expect of a six-year-old, in terms of an inventory of superficial characteristics. Instead of "I can run fast, my eyes are brown, and I hate broccoli," it's "I'm in three honors classes" or "my butt is way too big." If kids today have so much trouble locating their passion or finding their purpose, that really shouldn't be a cause for wonder.

But students, teachers have told me, never think of themselves as other-directed, just as parents never see themselves as *that* parent. When I suggested, at an event at Harvard, that college students need to keep an open mind about their decisions, one young woman replied, "We already made our decisions back in middle school, when we decided to be the kind of high achievers who get into Harvard." Leaving aside the question of whether you want to live forever with the decisions you made in seventh grade—or to put it another way, to let a seventh grader tell you how to live—one has to ask, in that context, just what "we" decided means.

Beyond the junior careerism, the directionless ambition, the risk aversion, and the Hobbesian competitiveness, the system cultivates a monumental cynicism. Whatever the motives out of which they were established, the old WASP admissions criteria actually meant something. Athletics were thought to build character—courage and selflessness and team spirit. The arts embodied an ideal of culture. Service was designed to foster a public-minded ethos in our future leaders. Leadership itself was understood to be a form of duty. Now it's all become a kind of rain dance that is handed down from generation to generation, an empty set of rituals known only to propitiate the gods. Kids do them because they know that they're supposed to, not because they, or anybody else, actually believes in them. If students were told that they needed to stand on their heads to get into Harvard, they would do so as eagerly, as diligently, as skillfully, and as thoughtlessly as they do everything else. The process takes activities that used to be ends in themselves and reduces them to means. No wonder they have also lost their souls: athletics means no more now than physical training; music means technical proficiency; service means charity; leadership means climbing to the top.

Experience itself has been reduced to instrumental function, via the college essay. From learning to commodify your experiences for the application, the next step has been to seek out experiences in order to have them to commodify. An article in the *New York Times* described the emergence of consulting companies devoted to producing essay-ready summers. What strikes one is the superficiality of the activities involved: a month traveling around Italy studying the Renaissance; three weeks in a creative writing program; two weeks as a counselor in a theater program; "a whole day" with a band of renegade artists. A whole day! "I love that and I got to put it on my application." (The artists were not quoted as to their impressions of the encounter, though I'm sure that they were glad to be of help.) The principal purpose of private admissions counselors, as Mitchell L. Stevens explains in *Creating a Class,* is to show students how to package themselves for consumption by admissions offices: which ultimately means, to create a self—or at least, the illusion of a self—that is capable of being packaged.

**If students have come to** be cynics about education itself; if they see it, as a Deerfield Academy graduate wrote me, as "not far from game theory, an algorithm to be cracked in order to get to the next level"; if they believe that "people don't go to school to learn," in the words of one of the students in *"Doing School";* if cheating has become endemic, and cheating scandals routine; then young people are only showing us what very good students they are, because they have learned the lessons we are teaching them. Why should it surprise us that they get to college having no idea why they're there, or that they run aground when called upon to make decisions for themselves, or that they prove to be such easy marks for recruiters selling answers?

We mandate "activities," so we reward joiners. We insist on "leadership," so we reward climbers. We value those who give us what we want, so we reward manipulators. We punish those who will not play the game. We are robbing children of their childhood and teenagers of their adolescence. We have engineered a vast regimentation of youth.

I know that there are lots of parents, even in the upper middle class, who don't conform to the Amy Chua model. Quite a few have said to me, essentially, I know better but I do it anyway. Just as there are many college students caught between conformity and courage, so are many parents struggling to do their best within a system that has lost its mind. But we need to do more than throw up our hands. We cannot continue to go with the flow, however powerful the current is. If we want our kids to turn out differently, we have to raise them differently.

# Four

## The Institutions

Fortunately, our colleges and universities are fully cognizant of the problems I have been delineating and take concerted action to address them. Curricula are designed to give coherence to the educational experience and to challenge students to develop a strong degree of moral awareness. Professors, deeply involved with the enterprise of undergraduate instruction, are committed to their students' intellectual growth and insist on maintaining the highest standards of academic rigor. Career services keep themselves informed about the broad range of postgraduate options and make a point of steering students away from conventional choices. A policy of noncooperation with *U.S. News* has taken hold, depriving the magazine of the data requisite to calculate its rankings. Rather than squandering money on luxurious amenities and exorbitant administrative salaries, schools have rededicated themselves to their core missions of teaching and the liberal arts.

I'm kidding, of course. None of this is happening, and none of it will happen without a fundamental change in the culture of higher education. Schools do little or nothing to wake students up from the values and habits they bring with them from high school—give little evidence, indeed, of recognizing there's a problem—which is why the undergraduate experience often ends up being nothing but more of the same. Kids are basically handed a course catalogue and told to figure it out for themselves. Yes, there are advisors, but they mainly serve to help students navigate the arcana of curricular requirements, as well as to usher them toward the counseling center if (I am tempted to say, when) the need occurs. Everything else is taken for granted, including the questions that might naturally be thought to arise in the course of forming an adult self and of undertaking the education that ought to assist one to do it.

Universities, writes Harry R. Lewis, the former Harvard dean, "have forgotten their larger educational role for college students": to help them figure out who they are and what their purpose in the world should be. Schools, in fact, "are having a hard time making the case that the education they offer is about anything in particular"—or as he puts it more bluntly, "Harvard no longer knows what a good education is." Curricula consist of long series of unrelated courses; distributional requirements follow the cease-fire lines of interdepartmental skirmishes. "There is no vision," writes Allan Bloom, "nor is there a set of competing visions, of what an educated human being is."

The problem is an old one, for its origins lie in the divided nature of American higher education itself. The American university inherits the missions of two very different institutions: the English college and the German research university. The first pattern prevailed before the Civil War. Curricula centered on the classics, and the purpose of education was understood to be the formation of character. With the emergence of a modern industrial society in the last decades of the nineteenth century, that kind of pedagogy was felt to be increasingly obsolete. Johns Hopkins was founded in 1876 as the first American university on the German model: a factory of knowledge that would focus in particular on the natural and social sciences, the disciplines essential to the new economy and the world to which it was giving rise. Other universities followed—the University of Chicago in 1890, Stanford in 1891—while existing institutions retooled themselves along the new lines. Soon the full structure of graduate research and education began to emerge: departments organized by discipline, national professional associations, peer-reviewed journals, publish-or-perish, the ladder of professorial ranks, tenure, dissertations, PhDs.

At the same time, and for the same reasons, Harvard was taking the lead in supplanting the old undergraduate curriculum with a system of electives and, eventually, of majors. College was now seen as preparation for professional life, the initial stage of specialization. But the old ideal of the liberal arts persisted, the notion that college should also speak to "the whole man": the concerns proper to an individual, not as a doctor or lawyer or scientist or manager, but as a human being—questions of purpose and value, as addressed above all, as their name implies, by the humanities. The years between the world wars saw a backlash against specialization, with schools developing a variety of "general education" curricula—most famously, the Great Books programs at Columbia and Chicago. The very fact that we still have majors at all in this country represents a compromise between the ideals of depth and breadth—not majors as opposed to nothing, but majors as opposed to nothing but. When someone studies chemistry, say, in England or France or just about anywhere else in the world, that is the only thing they study.

Great Books curricula came to grief in the 1960s and '70s, along with requirements in general. The Western classics were vilified as Eurocentric, mandatory courses as paternalistic. Brown, the "hot" college when I was graduating from high school in 1981, was famous for having done away with structure almost altogether. If the core curriculum has survived at Columbia, my alma mater, that is mainly, at this point, a matter of branding—something to distinguish the college's product from the competition's. What's left at most schools, for structure and breadth, are distribution requirements, a Chinese menu of columns A through C or D or F ("quantitative reasoning," "languages and literatures," "world cultures," and suchlike blandeurs) that offers students no coherence and often leaves them, as Bloom put it, "poking around for courses to take . . . just filling up their college years." The recent trend toward double majors can be seen, in part, as a tacit revolt against the formlessness of an elective system that can't remember why it exists. Specialization is the only part of the curriculum that makes sense to students anymore, so they might as well give themselves as much of it as they can.

But the ultimate problem lies deeper than cultural fashion or bureaucratic confusion. The foundational compromise of modern American higher education—the idea of housing a liberal arts college within a research university—has proved to be untenable. Because a single faculty exists for both, and because professors are trained and rewarded for research, the values of the university have inexorably won out over those of the college. The process took decades to unfold. For many years, at many schools, it was still possible to join the faculty without a PhD and to win tenure without much of a publication record. But professional norms have slowly tightened their grip. The boom in federal funding after Sputnik swung the balance of institutional power decisively toward research.

The collapse of the academic job market in the 1970s—the famous PhD glut, which never went away—meant schools could ratchet up their expectations for scholarly productivity. As knowledge is elaborated, research becomes ever more specialized. And because professors can teach what they want—which usually means their little square inch of the field, their thesis, their book—fragmentation and specialization have overtaken the undergraduate curriculum.

Nothing adds up because nothing is designed to add up. Professors don't care because they have no incentive to care. They want to do their research; they want to teach their research; and they don't want to have to think about anything else. The courses offered, Lewis says, do not bear any necessary relation to what students want or need to know. Efforts to look at the bigger picture—the periodic curricular reviews that faculty committees are convened to undertake—generally run aground on a mixture of territorialism, indifference, and simple incapacity. "We are just not accustomed to thinking about education in general terms," said Louis Menand, who cochaired a notably unsuccessful one at Harvard recently. "It's not our specialty."

Our leading colleges and universities pride themselves on their refusal to offer the kinds of vocational majors that most students opt for at most other schools, subjects like communications, business, education, and nursing, but everything they teach is vocational now, because of the spirit in which they teach it. Everything is technocratic—the development of expertise—and everything is ultimately justified in technocratic terms. Elite schools like to boast that they teach their students how to think, but all they mean at this point is that they train them in the analytic and rhetorical skills that are necessary for success in business and the professions. No more than in high school are students equipped to address the larger questions of meaning and purpose, about their education and their lives, that come so inevitably in young adulthood. Religious colleges, quite frankly—even obscure, regional schools that no one's ever heard of on the coasts—often do a much better job in that respect. What an indictment that is, of the Ivy League and its peers: that colleges four levels down on the academic totem pole, enrolling students whose SAT scores are hundreds of points lower than theirs, deliver a better education, in the highest sense of the word, than do those institutions.

But all is not lost. Elite schools still dimly recollect their responsibility to provide a general education, to teach the whole person, to be something more than expensive vocational schools. So when kids get to college, they hear a speech or two that urges them to ask the big questions. And when they graduate, they hear another speech or two that urges them to ask the big questions. And in between, they spend four years taking courses that train them to answer the little questions: specialized courses, taught by specialized professors, aimed at specialized students.

At least those classes are academically rigorous, demanding on their own terms, no? Not necessarily. In the sciences, usually; in other disciplines, not so much. At Harvard, Ross Douthat writes, academics were the easy part, "because almost no one seemed to be pushing back." There are exceptions, of course, and norms differ among institutions, but professors and students have largely entered into, in the words of one observer, a "mutual nonaggression pact." Students want to do as little as possible. Professors are rewarded for research, especially at elite schools, so they want to spend as little time on their classes as they can. To the extent that teaching matters at all for professional advancement, assessments are based almost entirely on student evaluations, which notoriously correlate with grades. For adjuncts and other people off the tenure track, an ever-larger share of teaching staffs, evaluations matter very much indeed. The answer, all around, is higher marks for shoddier work.

Grade inflation, and complaints about grade inflation, are an old story—as old as grades themselves, according to Lewis. Still, even if GPAs have been rising for more than a century, it makes a difference where they are. In 1960, the average GPA at private universities was about a 2.5. In 1990, it was about a 3.1. In 2007, it was 3.3, and at highly selective private schools, 3.43. Given the rate at which the numbers have been rising, the last figure is probably over 3.5 by now. The closer the curve gets squeezed to the ceiling, the harder it is to make distinctions and the less incentive students have to do their best. In 1940, 15 percent of grades fell within the A range; in 2008, the number was almost 45 percent. But there are always students who don't do the work, or who are taking a class outside their field (for fun, or to fulfill a requirement), or who are not up to standard to begin with (athletes, legacies). Grades are usually lower for freshmen, as well. At elite schools, at this point, if an upperclassman does the work, it is almost impossible to give them less than a B-plus, and even, increasingly, an A-minus.

But never mind the grades; it's even hard to give your students honest feedback. Kids who have been raised under a regimen of positive reinforcement, and whose self-esteem depends on perfection, are not well equipped to handle criticism. Besides, they have better things to do than hit the books. At a big, public party school—let's call it the University of Southern Football—that probably means beer and television. At elite colleges, it means those all-consuming extracurricular activities. Extracurriculars certainly have value: they're fun; they're social, which studying is not (at least, not if you do it right); they enable students to express and develop abilities that classes ignore; and they're good for making contacts and testing out vocational options. They also organize the campus social scene. But given kids' addiction to keeping busy, their fear of ever missing out on anything, they tend to expand to fill the available space.

The problem is, the more you do, the less you do well and the less well you do everything. A former student wrote an essay called "The Suckage Factor" as part of a packet for incoming freshmen. The suckage factor is a measure of how badly you suck at everything because you're trying to do too much. The figure is reached by dividing the number of hours in a day by the amount of time you spend on academics and activities:

> *Looking back on my first year, I can perform this calculation retroactively: as it turns out, I was allotting myself six minutes to read Homer's* Odyssey *and five minutes to scale Harkness tower for carillon practice, provided I slept two hours a night and ate lunch every second day. . . . Before long, I was pulling regular all-nighters in the library, but, paradoxically, not finishing my homework; I was running madly from meeting to rehearsal, but was never on time; I was thrashing about like a banshee in a whirlpool, and I was barely scraping by.*

The only way the system can work is for everyone, including professors, to lower their expectations. Elite students do indeed work incredibly hard, when you add it all up, and they're still as bright as ever, but that doesn't mean that the work they produce is necessarily up to the same standard. The reductio ad absurdum of the situation is embodied by the academic career of the actor James Franco, who has made a hobby of collecting graduate programs. At one point, Franco was enrolled at Columbia for writing, NYU for filmmaking, Warren Wilson for poetry, and Brooklyn College for fiction—all while maintaining a busy professional schedule. After graduating from Columbia, he started a master's in art at the Rhode Island School of Design and a PhD in English at Yale (yes, my old department). Franco, who went to Palo Alto High School, is a caricature of today's young high achievers. In college at UCLA, he was once allowed to register for sixty-two credit hours, the usual limit being nineteen. How can anybody be so brilliant, so talented, so energetic? They can't; they aren't: not him, not anyone. Getting into an elite college is harder than ever. But once you're in, the way things work today, all you need to do, to a significant extent, is just show up.

Yet there is also something operating here that runs much deeper than professorial laissez-faire or undergraduate angle-playing. The last thirty years or so has seen a revolution in the way that colleges think about their students. The decades after World War II had been a golden age for higher education. From 1949 to 1979, the number of students more than quadrupled, the number of faculty nearly tripled, and institutions were established at a rate of almost one a week. But as the baby boom aged out of college in the 1980s, schools were forced to scramble for students even while governments began to cut funding. Meanwhile, policy makers had initiated an effort to transform higher education into a consumer market by funneling money to students (through grants and loans) rather than to institutions.

The effort worked. Higher education increasingly resembles any other business now. What pays is in; what doesn't is under the gun. Instruction is regarded as a drain on resources. "Efficiency" in the transmission of knowledge, not the unscalable craft of teaching, has become the cardinal value. Professors are being replaced by adjuncts and other temporary, low-wage workers, the cost to educational quality be damned. Academic "units" (that is, departments) are seen as "revenue centers"; the ones that can't pull their weight—much of the liberal arts—are slated for downsizing or outright elimination. Science is king, but not just any science; basic research is suffering, too. The holy grail is technology transfer: scientific investigation, often sponsored directly by corporations, that is capable of being parlayed into profit. (So greedy have schools become in the pursuit of short-term revenue that even companies they seek to partner with have started to complain.) Continuous expansion is regarded as essential. New buildings, new research centers, new campuses around the world. NYU in Abu Dhabi, Yale in Singapore, Columbia in China, Turkey, Brazil: the point is to build the brand, capture market share, and tap the emerging sources of global wealth.

The "metric" everybody pays attention to, in the brave new world of academic management, is good old *U.S. News*. In the spirit of the SATs, in fact, we might propose the following analogy. *U.S. News* rank : schools : : SAT score : students. Each is dubious as a measure of academic excellence and meaningless as a standard of self-worth, but both have consequences serious enough to send their subjects into a state of panic. Colleges, in other words, are now being terrorized by the same sort of numerical regime they have long inflicted on high school students.

Yet if kids spend a lot of time (and their parents, a lot of money) trying to juice up their numbers, schools do far worse. "Selectivity" is a factor in the rankings, so colleges aggressively recruit more applicants, even though they know a lot of them have no chance of admission. Reputation is a factor, so schools sometimes lowball rivals in the survey that they all fill out. Average SAT scores are a factor, so institutions have been shifting their financial aid awards from need to merit—and since SAT scores correlate closely with family wealth, that means more money to kids who don't need it and less to those who do. And when all else fails, colleges, like students, simply cheat (by misreporting data), as has recently come out at Emory, Bucknell, Claremont McKenna, and other schools.

But the worst effect of the commercialization of higher education is the way that it has changed how institutions see their students. Now they think of them as "customers," people to be pandered to instead of challenged. You can fairly smell it on the campuses, where the students are so unmistakably in charge. Grade inflation, which shot up during the 1960s and early '70s, was largely flat from 1975 to 1990, but it has once again been on the rise since then. Not only do students now feel that they're paying for A's, but graduation rates are yet another consideration for *U.S. News*, so schools don't dare to flunk kids out. The customer-service mentality is also responsible for the profusion of swanky new dorms, gyms, and student centers—a building boom that, like the other ones that happened in the 1990s and early 2000s, was financed by a mountain of debt, and that has been a major factor in tuition growth. Colleges now sell themselves to kids in terms of what they can give them, not what they plan to expect of them. "With no larger educational ideals to shape the undergraduate experience," Lewis says, "decisions affecting students are calculated to satisfy their immediate demands." Instead of humanities, students are getting amenities.

Yet a commercial relationship is exactly the opposite of a pedagogical one. You give your customer what they want, but you don't have any interest in their long-term welfare. It is precisely because you do have an interest in your students' long-term welfare that you don't give them what they want. You question them, and the thing you question them about the most is what they want. Teaching, said Socrates, is the reeducation of desire. If that sounds paternalistic, it is. Professors should be mentors, not commodities or clerks. Education isn't something you consume; it's an experience that you have to give yourself over to. But colleges don't think like that anymore.

They see themselves as supplying a market, not guarding a public trust. If they no longer know what the education they offer is about, that's because they're waiting for their students to tell them.

**I have certainly known students** who feel they got a great education in college. But they always say some version of "the opportunities are there if you want to pursue them." In other words, you have to ask—or really, you have to insist. As Douthat wrote of his alma mater, "Harvard remains one of the best places on earth to educate oneself," but it "will not actively educate you, will not guide or shape or even push back in any significant way." In the words of Mark Edmundson, a professor at UVa, "To get an education, you're probably going to have to fight against the institution that you find yourself in—no matter how prestigious it may be. (In fact, the more prestigious the school, the more you'll probably have to push.)"

Think about that: you have to fight for what you came for, for what you're paying for. You can get it, but only if you insist on it. Imagine a hospital that operated on such a basis, or a grocery store. It's the kids who hope to get an education, not the ones who want to shirk the job, who find themselves confronting an inimical environment. More common, in my experience, than the intellectually serious student who felt fulfilled by their time in college is the one who left feeling cheated, wondering what it all added up to and what had happened to the sense of adventure with which they had entered four years earlier. I was often approached, during my years at Yale, by just that kind of kid: ardent, curious, independent— looking to college for meaning, not skills; looking to the world for possibility, not security. What they told me, invariably, was that they felt abandoned by their institution, that the education they were being offered had nothing to say to them and that they had no one to help them figure out how to live a life commensurate with their aspirations. These are the students that colleges should prize most highly, yet they are the ones that they're failing most badly.

The fact is that elite schools have strong incentives *not* to produce too many seekers and thinkers, too many poets, teachers, ministers, public-interest lawyers, nonprofit workers, or even professors—too much selflessness, creativity, intellectuality, or idealism. The most prestigious institutions do provide an abundance of academic, artistic, and moral opportunities, if only because they have the financial means to do so. A former student who started a creative writing program for inner-city children after college wrote me a long, impassioned letter about the ways that Yale provided her the resources to find and follow her path. But at the same time, colleges and universities do nothing to suggest that some ways of using your education are better than others. They do nothing, in other words, to challenge the values of a society that equates virtue, dignity, and happiness with material success.

Nor do they do much to help kids find their way to alternative careers. On the contrary: I've been told again and again, at school after school, that career service offices have little or nothing to say to students who are interested in something other than the big four of law, medicine, finance, and consulting. At the recruitment fairs, the last two dominate the field. And some schools go even further. Stanford offers companies special access to its students for a fee of ten thousand dollars—and it is hard to believe that Stanford is the only one.

Selling your students to the highest bidder: it doesn't get more cynical than that. But though the process isn't often that direct, that's basically the way the system works. As a friend of mine, a third-generation Yalie, once remarked, the purpose of Yale College is to manufacture Yale alumni. David Foster Wallace (Amherst '85), has a character put it like this:

> *The college itself turned out to have a lot of moral hypocrisy about it, e.g., congratulating itself on its diversity and the leftist piety of its politics while in reality going about the business of preparing elite kids to enter elite professions and make a great deal of money, thus increasing the pool of prosperous alumni donors.*

Of course colleges do nothing to discourage students from pursuing lucrative careers, no matter how personally unfulfilling or socially destructive. Of course they run a system that's designed to funnel students in exactly that direction. When James B. Conant, the president of Harvard, began the move toward meritocracy in the 1930s, he wanted to attract no more than a small minority of "remarkable talents"—the lion's share of spaces being still reserved for future businessmen, that is, donors. Now schools can have it both ways: the meritocrats *are* the future donors, as long as you select and train them right. Hence the increasing proportion of international students at elite colleges, as the scales of global economic power shift. The particular mix at places like Yale, I've been told, represents a form of geostrategic calculus. Kids from Western Europe are out; those from the BRICs (Brazil, Russia, India, and China) and other rising economies are in, the better to line up the major gifts a generation hence. As for the smattering of future artists and do-gooders, they're there to balance the moral books (as well as furnish a few alumni to brag about), not because of any strong commitment to beauty or justice.

For the most selective colleges, the system is working very well indeed. Application numbers continue to swell; endowments are robust; administrative salaries have jumped by leaps and bounds in recent years; tuition hikes bring ritual complaints but no decline in business. Whether it is working for anyone else is a different question. One of the saddest things for me in all of this is listening to kids in high school, or those who've just arrived at college, express their hopes for their undergraduate experience and knowing how likely they are to be disappointed. For despite it all, the romance of college remains: the dream, as Bloom puts it, of having an adventure with yourself. Beneath the cynicism that students feel they are forced to adopt, beneath their pose of placid competence, the longings of youth remain. There is an intense hunger among today's students, my travels in the last few years have shown me, for what college ought to be providing but is not: for a larger sense of purpose and direction; for an experience at school that speaks to them as human beings, not bundles of aptitudes; for guidance in addressing the important questions of life; for simple permission to think about these things and a vocabulary with which to do so. It is to the ways that they can start to satisfy that hunger that I now turn.

# PART 2

*Self*

# Five

## What Is College For?

"Return on investment": that's the phrase you often hear today when people talk about college. How much money will you get out of doing it, in other words, relative to the amount that you have to put in. What no one seems to ask is what the "return" that college is supposed to give you is. Is it just about earning more money? Is the only purpose of an education to enable you to get a job? What, in short, is college for?

We talk, in the overheated conversation we've been having about higher education lately, about soaring tuition, rising student debt, and the daunting labor market for new graduates. We talk about the future of the university: budget squeezes, distance learning, massive open online courses, and whether college in its present form is even necessary. We talk about national competitiveness, the twenty-first-century labor force, technology and engineering, and the outlook for our future prosperity. But we never talk about the premises that underlie this conversation, as if what makes for a happy life and a good society were simply self-evident, and as if in either case the exclusive answer were more money.

Of course money matters: jobs matter, financial security matters, national prosperity matters. The question is, are they the only things that matter? Life is more than a job; jobs are more than a paycheck; and a country is more than its wealth. Education is more than the acquisition of marketable skills, and you are more than your ability to contribute to your employer's bottom line or the nation's GDP, no matter what the rhetoric of politicians or executives would have you think. To ask what college is for is to ask what life is for, what society is for—what people are for.

Do students ever hear this? What they hear is a constant drumbeat, in the public discourse, that seeks to march them in the opposite direction. When policy makers talk about higher education, from the president all the way down, they talk exclusively in terms of math and science. Journalists and pundits—some of whom were humanities majors and none of whom are nurses or engineers—never tire of lecturing the young about the necessity of thinking prudently when choosing a course of study, the naïveté of wanting to learn things just because you're curious about them. "Top Ten Majors" means the most employable, not the most interesting. "Top Ten Fields" means average income, not job satisfaction. "What are you going to do with that?" the inevitable sneering question goes. "Liberal arts" has become a put-down, and "English major" a punch line.

I'm not sure what the practicality police are so concerned about. It's not as if our students were clamoring to get into classes on Milton or Kant. The dreaded English major is now the choice of all of 3 percent. Business, at 21 percent, accounts for more than half again as many majors as all of the arts and humanities combined. In 1971, 73 percent of incoming freshmen said that it is essential or very important to "develop a meaningful philosophy of life," 37 percent to be "very well-off financially" (not well-off, note, but very well-off). By 2011, the numbers were almost reversed, 47 percent and 80 percent, respectively. For well over thirty years, we've been loudly announcing that happiness is money, with a side order of fame. No wonder students have come to believe that college is all about getting a job.

You need to get a job, but you also need to get a life. What's the return on investment of *college*? What's the return on investment of having children, spending time with friends, listening to music, reading a book? The things that are most worth doing are worth doing for their own sake. Anyone who tells you that the sole purpose of education is the acquisition of negotiable skills is attempting to reduce you to a productive employee at work, a gullible consumer in the market, and a docile subject of the state. What's at stake, when we ask what college is for, is nothing less than our ability to remain fully human.

**The first thing that college** is for is to teach you to think. That's a cliché, but it does actually mean something, and a great deal more than what is usually intended. It doesn't simply mean developing the mental skills particular to individual disciplines—how to solve an equation or construct a study or analyze a text—or even acquiring the ability to work across the disciplines. It means developing the habit of skepticism and the capacity to put it into practice. It means learning not to take things for granted, so you can reach your own conclusions.

Before you can learn, you have to unlearn. You don't arrive in college a blank slate; you arrive having already been inscribed with all the ways of thinking and feeling that the world has been instilling in you from the moment you were born: the myths, the narratives, the pieties, the assumptions, the values, the sacred words. Your soul, in the words of Allan Bloom, is a mirror of what is around you. I always noticed, as a teacher of freshmen, that my students could be counted on to produce an opinion about any given subject the moment that I brought it up. It was not that they had necessarily considered the matter before. It was that their minds were like a chemical bath of conventional attitudes that would instantly precipitate out of solution and coat whatever object you introduced. (I've also noticed the phenomenon is not confined to eighteen-year-olds.)

Society is a conspiracy to keep itself from the truth. We pass our lives submerged in propaganda: advertising messages; political rhetoric; the journalistic affirmation of the status quo; the platitudes of popular culture; the axioms of party, sect, and class; the bromides we exchange every day on Facebook; the comforting lies our parents tell us and the sociable ones our friends do; the steady stream of falsehoods that we each tell ourselves all the time, to stave off the threat of self-knowledge. Plato called this *doxa*, opinion, and it is as powerful a force among progressives as among conservatives, in Massachusetts as in Mississippi, for atheists as for fundamentalists. The first purpose of a real education (a "liberal arts" education) is to liberate us from *doxa* by teaching us to recognize it, to question it, and to think our way around it.

In *Teacher*, Mark Edmundson describes the man who played this role for him when he was seventeen and thereby saved him from the life of thoughtless labor that appeared to be his fate. His teacher's methods were the same as those of Socrates, the teacher of Plato himself: he echoed your opinions back to you or forced you to articulate them for yourself. By dragging them into the light, asking you to defend them or just acknowledge having them, he began to break them down, to expose them to the operations of the critical intelligence—and thus to develop that intelligence in the first place. The point was not to replace his students' opinions with his own. The point was to bring his charges into the unfamiliar, uncomfortable, and endlessly fertile condition of doubt. He was teaching them not what to think but how.

Why college? College, after all, as those who like to denigrate it often say, is "not the real world." But that is precisely its strength. College is an opportunity to stand outside the world for a few years, between the orthodoxy of your family and the exigencies of career, and contemplate things from a distance. It offer students "the precious chance," as Andrew Delbanco has put it, "to think and reflect before life engulfs them." You can start to learn to think in high school, as Edmundson did—you're certainly old enough by then—but your parents are still breathing down your neck, and your teachers are still teaching to the test, in one respect or another. College should be different: an interval of freedom at the start of adulthood, a pause before it all begins. Is this a privilege that most young people in the world can only dream of? Absolutely. But you won't absolve yourself by throwing it away. Better, at least, to get some good from it.

College also offers you professors. Yes, it is theoretically possible to learn how to think on your own, but the chances are not good. Professors can let in some air, show you approaches that wouldn't have occurred to you and put you on to things you wouldn't have encountered by yourself. Autodidacts tend to be cranks, obtuse and self-enclosed. A professor's most important role is to make you think with rigor: precisely, patiently, responsibly, remorselessly, and not only about your "deepest ingrained presuppositions," as my own mentor, Karl Kroeber, once wrote, but also about your "most exhilarating new insights, most of which turn out to be fallacious." You want some people in your life whose job it is to tell you when you're wrong.

College also gives you peers with whom to question and debate the ideas you encounter in the classroom. "Late-night bull sessions" is another one of those phrases people like to throw at the college experience, a way of shaming students out of their intellectual appetites. But the classroom and the dorm room are two ends of the same stick. The first puts ideas into your head; the second makes them part of your soul. The first requires stringency; the second offers freedom. The first is normative; the second is subversive. "Most of what I learned at Yale," writes Lewis Lapham, "I learned in what I now remember as one long, wayward conversation in the only all-night restaurant on Chapel Street. The topics under discussion— God, man, existence, Alfred Prufrock's peach—were borrowed from the same anthology of large abstraction that supplied the texts for English 10 or Philosophy 116." The classroom is the grain of sand; it's up to you to make the pearl.

College is not the only chance to learn to think. It is not the first; it is not the last; but it is the best. One thing is certain: if you haven't started by the time you finish your BA, there's little likelihood you'll do it later. That is why an undergraduate experience devoted exclusively to career preparation is four years largely wasted. The purpose of college is to enable you to live more alertly, more responsibly, more freely: more fully. I was talking with a couple of seniors during a visit to Bryn Mawr. One of them said, "The question I leave Bryn Mawr with is how to put my feminist ideals into practice as I go forward." I liked "ideals," but I loved the first part. A real education sends you into the world bearing questions, not resumes.

**Learning how to think is** only the beginning, though. There's something in particular you need to think about: yourself. Liberal arts education is traditionally justified on the grounds of public interest, as a training in the skills of democratic citizenship. The classroom, in this conception, is a workshop of republican virtue: reasoned debate, principled dissent, respectful mutual engagement. There is much to be said for this idea, but it sells the enterprise extremely short. Before and beneath the public good that such an education does, there is a private one—we might say, *the* private one. "You're here for very selfish reasons," the legendary Columbia professor Edward Tayler would say to his freshmen the first day of class. "You're here to build a self." Whether this activity redounds to anybody else's benefit is, for the time being, beside the point. A self is something that you need to develop for your own sake, and it is not a quick or easy or even, often, a pleasant process.

Building a self: the notion may sound strange. "We've taught them," David Foster Wallace wrote about today's young people, "that a self is something you just *have*." It isn't that you don't have one at all, when you're a kid; there just is not a whole lot to it. In the words of the great Romantic poet John Keats, the world is a "vale of Soul-making." Not a "vale of tears," in the traditional phrase—a valley of sorrow that the soul is compelled to suffer through on its way to a salvation that lies *beyond* this world. And not a "soul" in the traditional sense, either, something eternal and unchangeable, somehow remote from and certainly other than our earthly self, and only involved, in any case, in matters of sin and virtue. By soul, what Keats meant *is* our earthly self, understood in its totality—moral, intellectual, sensual, emotional, our whole being. And by calling the world a vale of soul-making, he meant that experience itself is the crucible of its creation.

"Do you not see how necessary a World of Pains and troubles is," he wrote, "to school an Intelligence and make it a Soul?" (Necessary pains and troubles—helicopter parents, and those who wish to play it safe in general, take note.) The world is still a scene of sorrow, in Keats's conception, but also of pleasure and love and every other emotion: "a Place where the heart must feel and suffer in a thousand diverse ways." The heart feels, he says, and the intelligence is educated by reflecting on that feeling. Everyone is born with a mind, but it is only through this act of introspection, of self-examination, of establishing communication between the mind and the heart, the mind and experience, that you become an individual, a unique being—a soul. And that is what it means to develop a self.

So what does college have to do with it? College helps to furnish the tools with which to undertake that work of self-discovery. It's very hard, again, to do it on your own. The job of college is to assist you, or force you, to start on your way through the vale of soul-making. Books, ideas, works of art and thought, the pressure of the minds around you that are looking for their own answers in their own ways: all these are incitements, disruptions, violations. They make you question everything you thought you knew about yourself. "True liberal education requires that the student's whole life be radically changed," writes Allan Bloom. "Liberal education puts everything at risk and requires students who are able to risk everything." The process isn't comfortable, but it is exhilarating. There's nothing "academic" about it. If it happens right, it feels like being broken open—like giving birth to yourself. "An education," Lapham quotes an old professor, "is a self-inflicted wound."

I talked before about thinking your way beyond received opinion, *doxa*, and now I'm talking about thinking about yourself, but these are finally a single act. To change the way you look at the world is inevitably to change the way you look at your life, and vice versa. They are not even really separate things. Of all the beliefs we absorb before we're old enough to question them, the most powerful, as well as the most personal, are those that tell us who we are—that seek to determine our identity and our values. College is the place to start to determine them for yourself, to figure out, as the Columbia historian Mark Lilla has put it, "just what it is that's worth wanting." To find out not just who you wish to be, but who you are already, underneath what everyone has wanted you to think about yourself. To discover new ideals and new desires. To start to answer for yourself that venerable pair of questions: what is the good life and how should I live it?

The truth is that I don't particularly like the phrase "develop a meaningful philosophy of life" as a description of what you're supposed to do in college. For one thing, it's bloodless. "Develop a philosophy" sounds like you're composing a treatise. For another, it's static. You develop "a" philosophy, and then you carry it around in a box for the rest of your life, removing and applying it as needed. The process goes much deeper than that—it goes all the way down to the bottom—and it's incomparably more fluid and provisional. It doesn't stop the day you graduate, or really ever. Lapham's wound never heals, for the self that sustains it cannot return to a state of innocent unconsciousness. What you should really want to develop in college is the habit of reflection, which means the capacity for change.

I've been using the word *soul,* and though I'm not religious, I find that only a religious language has sufficient gravity to do these questions justice. For we are speaking of the most important thing: no less a thing than how to live. We might propose, then, that you should arrive at college as at the beginning of a pilgrimage—a movement toward the truth and toward the self. That you should come to seek conversion, though you know not yet to what belief or way. That you should approach ideas as instruments of salvation, driven by a need to work things through for yourself, so that you won't be damned to go through life at second hand, thinking other people's thoughts and dreaming other people's dreams. It's been said that people go to monasteries to find out why they have come, and college ought to be the same. We are born once, not only into nature but also into a culture that quickly becomes a second nature. But then, if we are granted such grace, we are born again. For what does it profit a man if he gains the whole world and loses his mortal soul?

Far from only training workers to contribute to the GDP, or even citizens to play a role within the public sphere, a true education, like a true religion, enables you to stand apart, and if necessary, against, the claims that others make upon you. The self is a separate space, a private space—exactly that inner space that Madeline Levine has found to be lacking in so many of her adolescent patients now. It is a space of strength, security, autonomy, creativity, play. You can live without a soul, D. H. Lawrence said, on ego and will alone—you can "go on, keep on, and rush on"—but you won't have very much inside you. People who behave like that, E. M. Forster has a character remark, are incapable of saying *I*. They cannot even say *I want*, "because 'I want' must lead to the question 'Who am I?'" So they only say *want*, without the *I*: "want money," "want mansion," "want Harvard."

In *Higher Education?*, Andrew Hacker and Claudia Dreifus remark that the purpose of college is to make you a more interesting person—a nice formulation, as long as we stipulate that the person to whom it is most important to be interesting is yourself, if only since that is the one with whom you have to spend the rest your life. But being interesting is very different from credentialed self-actualization, as David Brooks would call it. Being a quadruple major does not make you interesting. Editing the college newspaper while singing in an a cappella group, starting a nonprofit, and learning how to cook exotic grains—this does not make you interesting. Interesting is not accomplished. Interesting is not "impressive." What makes you interesting is reading, thinking, slowing down, having long conversations, and creating a rich inner life for yourself.

The purpose of college, to put all this another way, is to turn adolescents into adults. You needn't go to school for that, but if you're going to be there anyway, then that's the most important thing to get accomplished. That is the true education: accept no substitutes. The idea that we should take the first four years of young adulthood and devote them to career preparation alone, neglecting every other part of life, is nothing short of an obscenity. If that's what people had you do, then you were robbed. And if you find yourself to be the same person at the end of college as you were at the beginning—the same beliefs, the same values, the same desires, the same goals for the same reasons—then you did it wrong. Go back and do it again.

"I might as well get an education," Margaret Atwood has a character say. "That's how they talked about it, as if an education was a thing you got, like a dress." It should be obvious by now that the most problematic part of that idea is the word "you." "You" don't get an education. "You" is the variable in that expression. "You" is what an education operates *upon*. "Education's what's left over," goes the common jeer, "after you've forgotten everything you've learned." But the person who first formulated that idea was James B. Conant, the president of Harvard, and he did not mean it as a slur. Most of what you come across in college will inevitably fade from memory. What's left over, precisely, is you.

# Six

## Inventing Your Life

### I: Direction

Now self-knowledge is all well and good, but you still have to find a career, don't you? Of course you do, but that is half the reason that you need to know yourself. What are you good at? What do you care about? What do you believe in? Lara Galinsky, the author of *Work on Purpose*, speaks of the importance of asking such questions at "points of inflection," the junctures in life when you're making a choice about what to do next. The so-called pragmatism that seeks to rush young people past them, says William Damon in *The Path to Purpose*, is ultimately self-defeating, because you can't be happy if you don't know what you're working for. Self-knowledge is the most practical thing in the world, because it helps you find your way to a career that's right for you. "What is the meaning of life?" may be the stereotypical philosophical question, supposedly abstract and point-less, but it bares its teeth when you phrase it like this: "What is the meaning of *my* life?" That is not a question that you want to wake up asking when you're forty.

*Vocation* is Latin for *calling:* it means the thing you're called to do. It isn't something that you choose, in other words; it chooses you. It is the thing you can't *not* do. It makes more sense to you than you do—makes more sense *of* you. But the summons doesn't happen by itself. You have to do the work to make yourself receptive to it. To find yourself, you first must free yourself. You won't be able to recognize the things you really care about until you have released your grip on all the things that you've been taught to care about. And we already know, in the case of today's young high achievers, what those are.

I heard from a senior at Harvard who was writing her thesis on Harvard itself, how good it is at instilling self-efficacy, the sense that you can go out into the world and do whatever you want. There are some kids, she said, who get an A on a test and say, "I got it because it was easy," and there are other kids who say, "I got it because I'm smart." Although that sounded more to me like self-esteem, her point was that Harvard excels at producing the second kind of kid. I'd go even further, I replied: the kind of kid who goes to Harvard, or any selective college, is someone who already believes that about themselves. But there's another option, I continued. True self-esteem means not caring whether you get an A in the first place. It means recognizing, despite all you've been trained to believe, that the grades you get do not define your value as a human being. It means deciding for yourself what constitutes success.

She also claimed that Harvard students take their sense of self-efficacy out into the world and use it to be "innovative." But when I asked her what she meant by that, the example she produced was "being CEO of a Fortune 500." That isn't innovative, I said, that's just successful, and successful, again, according to a very narrow definition of the term. "Innovation" is all the rage these days, as a panacea for what ails us, but we need to innovate in our idea of innovation. You can invent a device or a drug or an app, but you can also invent your life. Instead of following a path, you can make your own path. There is artistic imagination, and scientific imagination, but there is also such a thing as moral imagination—"moral" meaning, not right or wrong per se, but having to do with the making of choices in the broadest sense. Moral imagination means the capacity to envision new alternatives for how to live. When you walk into a Starbucks, you are given a choice between a latte and a Frappuccino and a few other things, but you also have another option. You can turn around and leave; maybe what you really want is not there at all. When you walk into an elite college, you are offered a choice between medicine, finance, consulting, and maybe a few other things, but you do not have to order from that menu, either. You can even turn around and leave and think it over for a while.

Moral imagination is hard, and it is hard in a completely different way than the hard things that elite students are used to doing. You can't study for it. You can't compete for it. The qualities it calls upon are those of character, not intellect. It's never easy, and not only that, it's never enough. You also need courage, moral courage, the bravery to act on your imagination in the face of what your family and friends are going to say to try to stop you. Because they're not going to like it. The morally courageous person tends to make the individuals around him very uncomfortable. He doesn't fit with their ideas about the way the world is supposed to work, and he makes them insecure about the choices they themselves have made—or failed to make. Physical courage is admirable, but in social terms it's usually quite easy. You have your comrades there beside you, your community to cheer you on. Moral courage can be lonely indeed. People don't mind being trapped, as long as no one else is free. But stage a break, and everybody else begins to panic.

**I was speaking of these** matters to a class at Stanford. They happened to be reading *Middlemarch,* which is pretty much the ideal text with which to think them through. ("*Middlemarch,*" Virginia Woolf remarked, "the magnificent book which with all its imperfections is one of the few English novels written for grown-up people.") The novel's heroine is Dorothea Brooke, an ardent and idealistic young lady who wants to make her life significant. But the story is set in the 1830s in the English countryside, a time and place that offered little room for spiritual yearnings, especially on the part of young women. The best that she can do is try to realize her aspirations through her personal life. So instead of marrying the man that she's expected to, the handsome, bland Sir James (who ends up with her little cupcake of a sister, Celia), she horrifies her family and neighbors by opting for a rather formidable alternative, the Reverend Edward Casaubon. Casaubon is austere, dignified, learned, aged—a great mind, she thinks, whom it would be a privilege to assist in his intellectual labors.

He is also, as she soon discovers, sickly, petty, and emotionally frigid. She has made, it turns out, an enormous mistake. Life with Casaubon is lonely and bleak. When you don't play it safe, you really aren't playing it safe. But should she have married Sir James instead, and become a little wifey like her sister? Whatever one may think, there is little doubt what her creator, George Eliot, did. Dorothea is her hero, her great soul—the one person, of all the many figures in this teeming epic, who possesses both the imagination to conceive a different life and the courage to attempt to live it. So when she gets a second chance, a second choice, she doesn't play it any safer. This time she marries an idealistic young reformer, a man of no position whom her family finds even more objectionable. She will have to surrender her comfortable life—her lifestyle, as we'd say today—and go off to the city, as her sister puts it, to "live in a street." It is literally, for Celia, unimaginable. "How will you live?" she asks, as relatives always do. "You will go away among queer people. And I shall never see you. . . . And you will be so poor." Though Dorothea finally gets the life she wants, Eliot does not allow us to believe that it arrives without a cost. *Middlemarch* is indeed a novel for grown-up people.

But there's an even better instance of moral imagination and moral courage: George Eliot herself. In writing Dorothea's story, she underplayed, if anything, the drama of her own. She grew up in a place like the one she portrays in the novel, with nothing of her heroine's material advantages but every bit of her spiritual hunger and then some. She read intensely; she spent time with people who could teach her things; she thought for herself. When she announced that she had lost her religious faith, her father threatened to expel her from the house, but she refused to recant. Later on she moved to London, plunging into its literary life and daring to mix among men as an equal, behavior that was virtually unheard-of for a single woman.

And then she did something that was even more scandalous: she took up with a married man. Adultery was hardly as uncommon in Victorian England as we like to imagine. Her lover was already living in an open marriage, and his wife had children by another man. What Eliot did that was so outrageous was refuse to conceal it. She believed that love was more important than a legal contract, and she was determined to live openly with the man she insisted on calling her husband, even to the point of taking his name. And she suffered for it. She was shunned by society. Her older brother, whom she idolized, refused to talk to her. But she persevered. This was the life that she was going to live, and she wasn't going to apologize for it. Eventually, through sheer strength of will and genius—*Middlemarch* was immediately acclaimed as one of the greatest novels in the language— she forced the world to accept her on her own terms. But it took more than twenty-five years, and there were no guarantees that it was ever going to happen.

It's no surprise that when she came to write her masterpiece, she built it from these very themes: self and society, choice and consequence, cowardice and courage and convention and rebellion. Dorothea is not the novel's only character who means to "shape their own deeds and alter the world a little." The second-most important figure is a gifted young doctor named Lydgate, who plans to make a name in science. But Lydgate gets married too soon, to a vain and shallow beauty who insists on being pampered, and finally comes instead "to be shapen after the average"—an outwardly successful man who regards himself as a failure. For him, there is no happy ending. Lydgate has the imagination but lacks the courage, is finally too addicted to comfort and approval.

Yet that may be a little harsh. Lydgate must contend against the constraining effects of circumstance, as does everybody else within the novel. This is Eliot's highest theme, one she strikes before we meet a single character, in a meditation on the story of St. Theresa, the great religious reformer, with which the book begins. There are many potential Theresas, gifted souls, she says, but few can overcome the adverse conditions that surround them. Dorothea could have done better herself, if things around her had been different. "Tangled circumstance," Eliot calls it: a "web," to use the book's most famous image, that we weave and interweave for one another. Some decades later, in *A Portrait of the Artist as a Young Man*, James Joyce made use of a similar metaphor. "When the soul of a man is born in this country," the protagonist Stephen Dedalus says about

Ireland, "there are nets flung at it to hold it back from flight. You talk to me of nationality, language, religion. I shall try to fly by those nets."

Today we have other nets. "What are you going to do with that?" is a net. "Instead of finding your*self*, how about finding a job?"—that's a net. So is a term that I have heard again and again as I have talked with students about these things: "self-indulgent." "Am I being self-indulgent if I major in philosophy instead of something more practical?" "Isn't it self-indulgent to try to live the life of the mind when there are so many other things I could be doing with my degree?" "I want to travel for a while after I graduate, but wouldn't that be self-indulgent?" These are the kinds of questions that young people find themselves being asked today if they even think about doing something a little different—even worse, the kinds that they are made to feel compelled to ask themselves.

Look at what we have come to. We like to think of ourselves as a wealthy country, but it is one of the great testaments to the intellectual—and moral, and spiritual—poverty of American society that it makes its most intelligent young people feel that they are being self-indulgent if they pursue their curiosity. You're told that you're supposed to go to college, but you're also told that you are being self-indulgent if you actually want to get an education. As opposed to what? Going into consulting isn't self-indulgent? Going into finance isn't self-indulgent? Going into law, like most of the people who do, in order to make yourself rich, isn't self-indulgent? It's not okay to study history, because what good does that really do anyone, but it is okay to work for a hedge fund. It's selfish to pursue your passion, unless it's also going to make you a lot of money, in which case it isn't selfish at all.

"We think it odd that a man should devote his life to writing poems," the critic Dwight Macdonald said some years ago, "but natural that he should devote it to inducing children to breakfast on Crunchies instead of Krispies." I've had to talk a gifted young musician into acknowledging that music can make a difference in people's lives. It's considered glamorous now to drop out of a selective college if you want to become the next Mark Zuckerberg, but ludicrous to stay in to become a social worker. Everyone pays lip service to the notion of "making a difference" or "giving back," but altruism isn't given much support unless it is pursued prestigiously, and if possible, lucratively. Students are expected to demonstrate creativity and perform service in order to get into college, but no one thinks they should be dumb enough to take them seriously as vocational goals. Along with "self-indulgent" comes "sitting under a tree and writing poetry," an oddly specific stereotype that suggests that creative or intellectual work is invariably dreamy, solipsistic, irrelevant, useless, and maybe vaguely feminine and adolescent—as well as insisting, of course, that it isn't really work at all.

The pressure comes from all directions. A South Korean student told me that a passport agent dressed her down, right there at the airport as she was coming back for the summer, for wanting to study philosophy. "Now," a young woman who had gone to Harvard wrote me,

> *having graduated and found gainful employment at an independent bookstore, I'm encountering exactly the phenomenon you describe: the confusion and even indignation, among others, when I tell them I'm working at a bookstore, don't have immediate plans to go to grad school or law school, and don't aspire to be a lawyer or politician. Just last night, I had the same old fight with my dad: wasting a Harvard degree by learning to farm, cultivating real community, or giving myself time to think and*

*heal emotionally after years of severe compartmentalizing and backward socialization is worse than selling out—it's selfishness and laziness.*

It's easy for us to identify with the injured party here, the free spirit victimized by conventional attitudes, but we are far more likely to find ourselves on the other side of the argument. I know that I have been there, especially back in college and my early twenties, when friends began to go in directions that made me feel threatened because they represented values that I didn't understand. *We* are the ones, in other words, who are weaving the nets. "We insignificant people with our daily words and acts," says Eliot, "are preparing the lives of many Dorotheas."

So how do you find your vocation—or as people like to say today, your passion? That can be the hardest question that young people face, especially after being trained to think exclusively in terms of the next immediate goal. There are no easy answers, but here are a few suggestions. Do for work what you do spontaneously—or did spontaneously, back when you were younger, before all the spontaneity got beaten out of you. Do what you would choose to do anyway, even if you didn't get rewarded for it. Do the thing that you can immerse yourself inside for hours at a time. You know the thing you *wish* you could do, instead of what you're doing now? Just do that thing. Do what you love to do the most: no, not *that*—not what you think you love, or think you ought to love, but what you really do love.

There is by now a robust literature on the nature of happiness, and it converges on a pair of observations. Beyond a moderate level of material comfort, happiness consists of two things: feeling connected to others and engaging in meaningful work. These are hardly new ideas. Aristotle, who said that man is a social animal, also said that happiness derives from exercising one's particular capacities. Doing strenuously, in other words, what you do well. Summoning that sense of joy and freedom that arises from your belly when you're doing work that calls upon your favorite powers.

I was talking to an intro philosophy class at Claremont McKenna, an extremely practical place where half the students major in economics or government. Why were they taking the course? Because it fulfills a requirement, a lot of them said. Okay, but is it fun? Yes, they almost all agreed, it was. So what does that mean? I asked. "Well," said one, "it's not what people usually mean by 'fun.' It lets me think about the things I want to think about." Another said, "I can lose myself in the material for hours." Exactly, I said. Some people will have that experience with philosophy, some people will have it with math, but "fun" is what all your classes should be, or as many of them as possible, and it's also what your work should be, if you can manage it.

The point is eminently practical. Not everyone's equipped for the kinds of quantitative fields that college students are typically urged to enter. There's no use going into engineering if you aren't very good at it. You'll learn more, do better, try harder, and be more successful if you study something that you're interested in. "From a very early age, perhaps the age of five or six," George Orwell wrote, "I knew that when I grew up I should be a writer. Between the ages of about seventeen and twenty-four I tried to abandon this idea, but I did so with the consciousness that I was outraging my true nature." You don't want to outrage your true nature. In *The Top Five Regrets of the Dying*, a nurse who works in end-of-life care reports that the single most common regret her patients express is that "I wish I'd had the courage to live a life true to myself, not the life others expected of me." You can endlessly delay gratification, doing work you hate because of the promise of future reward, or you can find your way to work that is its own reward.

Lara Galinsky warns against placing too much emphasis on "passion," in talking to young people, because the word can be intimidating. A lot of them will say, as I have often heard myself, that they aren't really sure that they do have a particular passion. Galinsky prefers "purpose," and I certainly have no quarrel there. In fact, it is probably best not to fetishize any particular word. I have also used "vocation" here, and I recognize that that can be intimidating, too. Not everybody hears a call, or maybe you feel called in several different ways and are having trouble sorting out which one to pursue. "Purpose," William Damon says, has the virtue of uniting the inner with the outer, the self with the world: what you want to do with what you see as needing to be done. "What moves you?" Galinsky likes to ask. "What do you feel connected to?" Becoming a lawyer isn't a purpose. Becoming a lawyer to defend the rights of workers, or to prosecute criminals, is. Purpose means doing something, not "being" something.

Purposeful work is spread out all along the income distribution. According to a study Damon cites, "Bus drivers, nurses, clerks, and waitresses were just as likely to find meaning in their work as people in 'elite' professions such as law and medicine." One thing is certain, he stresses: money and status are not enough for a sustaining purpose, and neither is the so-called realist's goal of "just earning a living"—the problem being exactly with that "just." Next time someone tells you that you should forget about finding a sense of meaning or doing what you love and just worry about earning a living, ask yourself if that's what they did. Chances are it's not, and if it is, ask yourself if they seem like a happy person.

•　　•　　•

**David Brooks has criticized the** "expressive individualism" that counsels graduates to "find yourself" or "follow your dreams" as nothing more than "baby-boomer theology." It is a great deal more than that. However often it is cheapened, sentimentalized, or reduced to a cliché or a marketing device, it is a basic idea, perhaps *the* basic idea, both of modern life and of that quintessentially modern country, the United States. It is Emerson's self-reliance and Thoreau's injunction to step to the beat of your own drummer. It is the theme of the lion's share of classic novels: the drama of coming of age, of developing a self and finding a place in the world.

It is also an inevitable response to the modern condition. In traditional society—where the meaning of your life was determined by external structures of belief, where your place in the world was within your community, and where you simply did the kind of work that your father or mother had done—there was no need to think about those things and no opportunity to change them. Now we have the gift and burden of freedom: the chance to figure them out for ourselves. We can surrender that chance and let other people tell us what to do—freedom is often scary and confusing—but we shouldn't pretend that it doesn't exist. The problem is not that we believe in finding yourself and following your dreams; the problem is that we aren't equipping our children to do it, and that maybe we're not sure we want them to.

But Brooks is still at least half right. "Most people don't form a self and then lead a life," he says. "They are called by a problem, and the self is constructed gradually by their calling." The first part is certainly true. You don't sit in your dorm room and create a self. College is only the start of the process, and the capacity for introspection that college should develop is only one of the things that you'll need. But I do find Brooks's notion of a "problem" problematic. It happens that way sometimes, as seems especially the case for some of the more adventurous young people today, the kind who are attracted to social entrepreneurship. Municipal governments need to become more efficient, so you write an app that connects people to local services. Poor communities have trouble getting healthy food, so you create a service program that helps to bring fresh produce into schools.

But what about other kinds of entrepreneurship? If you make a computer game, or start a design business, or set up shop as a baker, are you solving a problem or taking advantage of an opportunity? What about the professions: teaching, nursing, social work, academia, the clergy, as well as law or medicine? People are often drawn to them as much for the intrinsic nature of the work they involve (I like little kids; I'm obsessed with archeology; I feel close to God) as for their larger ends. What about creative work? Writing a song is not a response to a problem or even, really, to an opportunity; it arises from an inner compulsion, a need to express and communicate. Brooks himself is a journalist, political commentator, and social critic. I don't know how he would describe the impulses that have driven his career, but I would guess that they involve a combination of intellectual curiosity, philosophical beliefs, and moral passions, not the desire to solve a problem. I'd bet he even found himself and followed his dreams.

One word, oddly, that is never used in this connection is "ideals." Justice, beauty, goodness, truth—the old moral lodestars. We seem to find the word forbidding now, preferring the squishier "values." But ideals have enormous power. They give you the strength to resist the seductions of status and wealth and success. An ideal is something that is more important to you than anything the world can give you. It functions the way that religious belief once commonly did, and in fact I've found that religious students are often the ones who possess the greatest degree of moral autonomy, are most indifferent to outside approval. "Ideals are psychological goals," the critic Alfred Kazin wrote, "necessary to the health of the mind." And although you are expected to discard them at the college gates the day you graduate, Franklin Delano Roosevelt wrote to his old headmaster forty years later, during the darkest days of World War II, to thank him for urging him to hold fast to his youthful ideals in later life.

I've spoken with a lot of recent graduates over the last few years, young people who are making their way through their twenties, coming to realizations that they wish they'd had in college but persevering in figuring out who they are and what they want to do. Here are a couple of their stories:

Eunice is an Asian-American woman in her late twenties whom I met at a Yale alumni event to which I'd been invited. She grew up in the suburbs of Seattle, majored in economics, and went to work for Morgan Stanley after graduation. She got a lot of academic mentorship at college, she said, but no career mentorship. "When you're graduating," she told me later in a follow-up interview, "you only have certain options unless you're willing to do it yourself, because career services doesn't help." Most of her friends went into law, medicine, or business. Everyone seems to be doing the same thing, she said, and the least happy are the ones who went to law school. Very few are doing something "amazing," something that she looks at and says, "I want to be doing that."

Eunice left Morgan after three years, the first time she had ever quit anything. "I was afraid if I stayed in and I was happy with the money, I would never leave." She went to work in Shanghai, where she found a hodgepodge of people among the young Americans there. Not all of them had gone to elite schools, but all were enjoying their lives a lot more than the people she had graduated with. The common factor was a willingness to accept risk. They ran restaurants, worked as writers, were entrepreneurs: a young woman who had started a production company, an event planner, someone running a cupcake business. It was the first time she had ventured out of "the Ivy League bubble," encountering people who hadn't gone to those kinds of schools but were still successful.

After two years in Shanghai, Eunice returned to Seattle, where she was taking a year off to catch her breath and think things over. She was training as a yoga teacher just for fun, volunteering in areas that interested her, and planning to start an MBA in the fall. She knew that business school could be as narrowly directed an experience as college, but now she was ready to be proactive about finding a nontraditional path. Looking back, she wishes she had majored in something more interesting instead of defaulting to economics. "College is not about getting a job," she had discovered, "it's about getting an education." But the whole process as it currently exists, she added, does not allow you to be "inward-turning"—"to think about what you *really* want instead of what you *think* you want."

She had more perspective now on other things, as well. "When you graduate from Yale, you feel the pressure to have another blue-chip name on the resume," she said. "But really, who's looking?" Now she cares a lot less about what people think. Material possessions are less important, too, "sanity" a lot more. She had been working twelve-hour days at Morgan, but "it doesn't make sense to be in the rat race if your heart is not in it," she said. "You need to be happy when you go home." There's a difference between the things you desire, she told me, and the things you need to live what she beautifully called "a sustainable life."

Now a second story, this time in the person's own words. Margaret wrote me after reading one of my essays:

*I think I fell into the exact traps you outlined: without wanting to be, Columbia made me competitive, made me feel self-indulgent for wanting to travel/volunteer my way through the end of my savings after graduation. So though that had been my plan (and dream) all throughout college, I ended up feeling guilty when all my peers were actively job seeking. In the end, I "compromised" with myself—settling for a prestigious fellowship at a globally renowned research institute, as a visiting researcher on climate change and agriculture. At least, I told myself, it was located abroad, in somewhat "exotic" tropical Brazil.*

*But during my time here, seeing senior researchers battle for directorship roles, talking smack about people who "only" have two Masters degrees (rather than a proper PhD), and feeling trapped in an office writing about issues in faraway lands I've never even set foot in, I've continually thought about your article. And I've realized: I'm pretending. I'm pretending to be a climate scientist (in reality, I studied international relations, which itself was an excuse to be abroad as much as possible while still graduating in four years). And I'm pretending to care about this job that I know hundreds would kill for. (A few months ago, I received a request from an African PhD candidate to be my intern. . . .) But most of all, I'm pretending to care about this version of "success." Because in reality, what Ivy League–caliber schools like Yale or Columbia teach their students is how to pretend, and how to do it well. And I do it damn well. I've been promoted here and offered raises; I've been published in scientific journals and given the keynote address at an international research conference. I'm good at what I do, but ultimately, it's just what I do, not what I love. And so I've done some soul-searching to really think about the kinds of "smart" I'd like to be, and the kinds of skills I really have (and don't just pretend to have). And I've realized that I don't want to climb the* *ladder of "success"; in reality, maybe all I want is to have a small non-profit restaurant that never really exceeds a capacity of 30. And it's a crazy idea; I'm 22 and have limited capital, and I'd like to do it in South America. But together with another disillusioned Ivy League graduate (Cornell '11), we're going to try it. And in the process of working out the kinks, we're realizing all the things a $55,000/year education didn't teach us—like how the hell you properly prime a wall, or build a wooden table from cheap wood, or balance a restaurant budget. And if we fail epically, at least we had the "moral courage" to give it a shot.*

Eunice is a pragmatist who wants to do something more interesting with her life. Margaret is a dreamer who is willing to take a big chance. Eunice is moving in the direction of greater service to society. Margaret probably sounds like she is moving in the opposite direction, and there may be many who would question her choice (as well as her willingness to throw away such a seemingly great opportunity). What they have in common is a desire to do what they feel they want to do, not what they're "supposed to do" in any sense, whether that means making a lot of money or saving the world.

**And now a final story:** mine. My path was long to recognizing my vocation, much longer than it had to be. My father was a professor of engineering; my older siblings were health professionals already, or well on the way, by the time I started college. Science was the horizon of possibility in my family; nothing else counted or even existed. Add to that the expectation of professional success that came with being the child of Jewish immigrants, and no matter how much I loved to read and write, it literally never occurred to me to major in anything else.

I had also loved biology in high school, thanks to two terrific teachers, and had long been curious about psychology, so when I saw in the catalogue orientation week that Columbia offered a joint major in the two fields, I chose it on the spot. No wait-and-see, no exploration of the new worlds of thought whose names the catalogue whispered (anthropology, history, classics), no investigation of what the major even entailed, beyond a list of courses. The feeling, other than excitement, was one of relief. I couldn't bear the uncertainty that college represented. Instead of opening options up, I needed to shut them down. And shut them down I did. Between the major, which was more like a major and a half, and Columbia's core curriculum and other requirements, I had locked up three-quarters of my courses for the next four years, and I hadn't even gone to a single class.

There was no one there to stop and make me think, no one there to save me from myself. My freshman composition teacher, whose class I loved and who might have provided a modicum of mentorship, did not bother to suggest that I ought to consider pursuing my passion for language. I don't know when exactly things began to go wrong with my chosen course of study, or why. Perhaps there was simply a natural limit to my interest, or perhaps it had to do with the way that all the science classes were taught, in large lectures with no discussion sections, or perhaps my vision of what I was going to do with it all, why I was slogging through what turned out to be a lot of dry material, was too vague to sustain me. I would mope in the back of those lectures, reading a novel behind my notebook, oblivious to the fact that I was trying to tell myself something.

By the time I realized that I should have been an English major, it was too late to make the switch. But what was I going to do with my life? Like a lot of people then, I bolted for the safety of law school. I went to Stanley Kaplan's, took the LSATs, applied to a bunch of schools—but stopped myself from going after it occurred to me to wonder, surprisingly late in the game, whether I actually wanted to be a lawyer. Instead, I went to school for journalism, a field in which I'd done some extracurricular dabbling, but only because it gave me a place to park myself for a year, and after all—another attitude that I'd unconsciously absorbed—what else *was* there to do after college, if not go to some kind of grad school? But that was predictably miserable, too; I didn't want to be a journalist, either, and afterward the only place that even interviewed me was a tiny, dying nonprofit. So there I was, a couple of years after college, bitter from the fact that I had thrown away the chance to get an education, working a job that meant nothing to me, my career essentially dead in the water, my self-belief in ruins, with no idea what I wanted to do or where I should go next.

And then I happened to be visiting a friend in architecture school. She wasn't happy, either; her program was way too pretentious and theoretical. We were walking along—I can practically point to the spot where it happened—and she said, "I have to get out of graduate school." And I immediately thought—it was a totally irrational response, of course—"I have to go to graduate school." Meaning, I'll never be happy until I give myself the chance to study English after all. Meaning, goddam it, it's not too late—I'm not going to let it be too late. That was it: that was the lightning bolt. Everything was suddenly clear and calm. I understood what I needed to do, because I'd let myself become aware of what I'd always known.

It wasn't easy getting in at that point. I was rejected by something like nine of the eleven programs I applied to, and the ones that did admit me were going to make me fight to keep my place by cutting half the class at the end of the initial year. But for the first time in a very long while, I performed at the top of my ability, and for the first time ever, I loved being in school. I'd study for seventy, eighty hours a week, reading until 4 A.M. in my crummy little room in graduate student housing, and I had never been happier. I had finally learned to listen to my gut, or in more sophisticated terms, had come to recognize the moral significance of desire. I had found out that I could do what I wanted, and that I could do it just because I wanted to.

## II: Risk

In order to invent your life, you need to overcome that thing the system is so good at inculcating: fear of failure. Damon repeatedly stresses the importance, not of avoiding failure, but of learning to cope with it as a normal and valuable part of development. The best reason to fail is to learn that failure isn't the end of the world. "The first time I blew a test," I sometimes say to campus groups, "I walked out feeling like I no longer knew who I was. The second time, it was easier." The statement never fails to elicit a round of cathartic laughter. Students are relieved to discover that it's possible to blow a test or two and still survive to adulthood. When Drew Gilpin Faust, the president of Harvard, was asked to name a book that she wished that all her incoming freshmen would read, she cited Kathryn Schulz's *Being Wrong*, which "advocates doubt as a skill and praises error as the foundation of wisdom." Never to have failed is a sign not of merit but fragility; it means your fears have kept you from doing or becoming what you might have. "Fail better," Samuel Beckett famously wrote. If your standards are as high as they should be, you will fail again and again. That is the difference between

mere success—getting the A, measuring up to some generic bench-
mark that may not actually be very high at all—and true excellence.

But there is also failure in a larger sense, and you need to be
prepared for that, as well. I mean the kind that Dorothea suffers in
*Middlemarch:* big mistakes, existential mistakes. "I am not afraid
to make a mistake," Stephen says in *Portrait of the Artist,* "even a
great mistake, a lifelong mistake, and perhaps as long as eternity
too." Those are powerful and moving words, and they have long in-
spired me, but we need to take them at their full weight. The wager
paid off for Joyce (though we don't know if it did for Stephen), but
that doesn't mean it will for you. For every person who takes the
risk of going their own way and ends up accomplishing remarkable things—for every George Eliot or Steve Jobs—there are very
many who fall short. The reason to try, the reason to invent your
life—whether you aim at remarkable things or only at your own
thing—is so that it will be *your* life, *your* choice, *your* mistakes. As
a colleague of mine once said, if kids got off the treadmill that takes
them to Wall Street, they would still make mistakes, but at least
they wouldn't all make the same mistake. Of course you'll make
mistakes, and some will be hard to endure. But life is finally a long
process of learning how you ought to have lived in the first place. Or
it is if you do it right.

In mentoring young social entrepreneurs in her role as senior
vice president of Echoing Green (a leading funder of social start-
ups, the organization has provided seed money to Teach For America, City Year, and hundreds of others), Lara Galinsky talks about
the importance of "willful naïveté." You kind of have to close your
eyes to the feeling that you're trying to do the impossible. Imagination means, by definition, that you're bringing something new into
the world. It only feels impossible because nobody's ever done it
before—or at least, you never have.

You must, in other words, face down your fears. Fear, a high school teacher said to me not long ago, is an agent of control, something that authorities instill to make you tractable. And the biggest boogeyman whose name is whispered to our future high achievers is "the gutter." It's either Harvard or the gutter—that all-or-nothing mentality again. "I hope you're happy being a *plumber*," they used to say when we were kids, if you showed the slightest sign of weakening resolve. To hear some of my young correspondents talk, the only alternatives are writing novels in a basement (that is, the life of the mind) or trading derivatives in a glass tower (the life of prudent practicality). It's a ridiculous notion, of course, and once you press on it a bit, once you push back against the fear instead of going into a defensive crouch, the argument collapses.

Galinsky quotes her mother, who was definitely not the kind of parent who tries to scare her kids away from risk. "Fear means go," she would say: some fears are legitimate, but the ones that are born from insecurity are signals telling you to march resolutely toward them. Parents tend to forget what it's like to be young, what youth can endure and achieve. How often have I heard of people telling their children not to take exactly the same kinds of risks—whether personal or professional, about work or sex or whatever—that they not only survived just fine themselves, but that made them who they are.

**The dull predictability of prescribed** elite career paths is, if nothing else, repugnant as a moral spectacle. Never to have tasted the pleasures; always to have played it safe. Never to have thrown your life upon the scales; always to have been sober and orderly. Never to have followed an ideal; always to have been sure of yourself. Who wants to live like that? Far better to resist the temptation to security. Emerson quotes Oliver Cromwell: "A man never rises so high as when he knows not whither he is going." The desire to eliminate uncertainty eliminates life.

I think of Meryl Streep, who has talked about awakening to feminism during her years at Vassar in the early 1970s. ("It was an emergence, which is what you hope for for a kid when they go off to college.") I think of the acclaimed lesbian cartoonist Alison Bechdel, how her friends turned her on to Adrienne Rich, who wasn't yet on any syllabus. I think of Patti Smith, taking fire at her first encounter with the French poet Rimbaud, whose work and life have been an inspiration for so many young seekers. ("He possessed an irreverent intelligence that ignited me.") I wonder how often this sort of thing still happens. How often *can* it happen? Do young people still have the chance, do they still give themselves the chance, to experience the power that ideas have to knock you sideways, into a different life? How likely are they to surrender to the kind of serendipity that Jobs talked about as having been essential to his own development? Is there still an underground of secret knowledge among the young, the blueprints for a project of self-reconstruction?

Or are they more likely to remain under the supervision of what the writer Rick Perlstein has called "the bureaucracy that schedules students' self-exploration"? I was speaking with a student who was planning to become a judge. (She was also thinking about taking a year off before law school, but only one, and only if she could do something "productive.") She was an intellectually serious young woman, but only within limits. "Each book I read," she reminisced about her first couple of years at school, "totally changed my world-view." But not, I ventured to note, her life plan. She was taken aback—it had apparently never occurred to her that their ought to be a relationship between the two—then explained that she had "just known" what she had wanted to do since ninth grade.

It is certainly true that some people are blessed enough to be able to recognize their vocation at an early age (a phenomenon that seems to be more common in creative fields). But there are differences between someone like Orwell, for example, and my junior justice. Orwell had already had some tangible experience of what the work of writing involves: "I had the lonely child's habit of making up stories and . . . I knew that I had a facility with words and a power of facing unpleasant facts." Being a writer is not the kind of "summit" occupation people tend to covet for its status (though the glamour that surrounds it ought to be a reason to think twice). Above all, as we saw, he reconsidered the idea during, precisely, his years of young adulthood. He went and lived for a while, and when he circled back to his original conviction, it was with the judgment and self-knowledge of an incomparably maturer person.

Another colleague has remarked that today's young people belong to a "post-emotional" generation—that they prefer to avoid feelings that are too chaotic and powerful. I don't know if that is true, but I do believe that it's essential not to shy away from the challenging parts of the self—not to deny the impulses and doubts that threaten to knock you from your charted path. The archetypal wanderer in Western literature is Odysseus; indeed the title of his poem has become synonymous with the life-changing, soul-making journey. Odysseus roams for a decade, experiencing a world of gods and monsters that lies beyond his imagination and being tested to the limits of his strength and ingenuity. He is rescued, at last, by Athena, his protector. But the figure who had sent the storm that blew him off course to begin with, all those many years before, was no one other than Athena herself. She saves him, eventually, but she also knows that the best thing she can do is push him into the sea in the first place—into the turbulence, into the tracklessness—to force him to improvise and change direction and discover what the world contains, and what he does.

•   •   •

**I cannot emphasize enough that** inventing your life does not come without potential costs. People say "find your passion," but they don't say "be prepared to suffer" (if only by surrendering the status that you might have had). They say "follow your dreams," but they don't say "the hell with credentials." I don't mean credentials per se, which are obviously often necessary, but credentialism, that lust for prestige that more or less defines the elite mentality and makes it impossible to find your passion or follow your dreams. How absurd it is—how disgusting, really—for commencement speakers to get up and mouth those exhortations at the very schools that do so much to preclude their fulfillment.

Status is a funny thing. Money gets you stuff, at least. Status doesn't get you much except the knowledge that you have it. And while money may not make you happy, it is easy to imagine someone who decides they have enough. With status, you can never have enough. It is comparative, and competitive, by its very nature. It doesn't just not make you happy: it actively makes you unhappy. You want to make it to the top? There is no top. However high you climb, there is always somebody above you. Mailer wanted to be Hemingway, Hemingway wanted to be Joyce, and Joyce was painfully aware he'd never be another Shakespeare. And so it goes in every field. I can tell you right now where you're going to end up: somewhere in the middle, with the rest of us. Does it really matter exactly where? People get to places like Yale and think that they've "arrived," only to discover that there are still other places to arrive at, and other places after that, and so on and so forth in an infinite recession, like the vista in a double mirror. As for why we cling to status in the first place, the answer seems to lie very deep in our psyches, down there with honor and shame and pollution, with ego, self-image, and self-esteem. Even money finally seems to matter mainly as a way of getting it.

I was talking to an audience at Stanford. Following your passion means, by definition, giving something up, I said, and what you might have to give up is Stanford: getting in, or if you're already there, getting in to "Stanford" at the next level. The idea, needless to say, did not go over very well. I have heard from many high-achieving students who have asked me whether it wasn't possible to be invested both in learning for its own sake and in being at the top. No, I've said, it isn't possible. Learning for its own sake means exactly what it says: learning is the only reason that you're doing it, because learning is what matters. Wanting to be at the top involves a rather different set of motivations, and you need to look that in the face. Can you get there anyway, simply as an accidental outgrowth of your efforts? Maybe, but do you really mean accidental, or are you trying to sneak behind your own back?

I would be the last person to suggest that overcoming the need for status, for success in the eyes of the world, is an easy thing to do. It's an addiction, which means you never really do get over it. The best that you can do is learn to manage it. I often think, in this regard, of Alcoholics Anonymous, how you're supposed to go to meetings every day, because you need to remember what you're up against, and gather the strength to fight it, every day. You may never completely eradicate the need for status, but you do not have to act on it. And the more that you resist it, the weaker it becomes.

Instead of success, make the work itself the goal. That's what I always come back to. When I start to care too much about rewards, I remember to return to the work—to the never-ending effort to perfect it. Just put your head down and forget about everything else: happiness has come to me when I have done that, misery and false directions otherwise. "Everything undertaken for its own sake is worthwhile," the writer Geoff Dyer has put it, "irrespective of the outcome." And the best part is, it's in your hands. Whether you get the recognition you think you deserve is out of your control, but the task itself is not. Aim high, to be sure, but do it for the love of the work. The work and the love—that's all that's going to be there in the end in any case. The only real grade is this: how well you've lived your life.

I am painfully aware that much of what I've been saying has long been reduced to cliché—and worse than cliché, advertising fodder. "Be yourself," "Do your own thing," "You only live once": such sentiments are next to meaningless by now. Everything is "edgy" today; everyone's creative or an innovator or an innovative creator who thinks outside the box. Thomas Frank and others have been telling us for years about commodified dissent and the rebel consumer. Slacks, sneakers, soft drinks, songs—all are packaged with the promise that they'll make you stand out from the herd, along with everybody else who buys them. We're told to "Change the Script," "Chart Your Own Course," and, of course, "Think Different." The great exponents of American individualism have been exhumed, as in a kind of voodoo, for the purpose of selling us pants: Levi's has given us Whitman ("Pioneers! O Pioneers!"); Gap has told us that Kerouac wore khakis. The timid practicality that is the major message that our kids absorb today is alibied—and camouflaged, and soothed—with a hollow commercialized rebellion.

You need to avoid that kind of crap. Putting a sticker on your MacBook that says "I'm an individual" (in whatever paraphrase) does not make you an individual. Getting a piercing, growing a mustache, moving to Austin—these do not make you an individual. You can't accessorize your way to moral courage. The choices it involves are not consumer ones. Cool furniture and hip music are perfectly nice, but they are utterly beside the point. Facebook also doesn't count; you don't become an independent thinker by posting quotes from independent thinkers. Here's a rule of thumb: if you aren't giving anything up, it isn't moral and it isn't courage. Stumbles, sacrifices, inner struggle, false starts and wrong turns, conflict with parents and peers—these are some of the signs of the genuine article. The way you know it's real is if it hurts.

Don't fake it. I knew somebody who'd been unconventional in college and was still living off the fumes of it a decade later, still posing as a rebel, as she flung herself into the most numbing conformity. It's important to maintain your ideals in college, but they probably won't be tested until later, sometimes quite a few years later, when and if you start to act on them in ways that go beyond words and gestures and really force you to put things on the line. Don't do it to be cool, either. That only means you've substituted the approval of your peers, or some of your peers, or an imaginary audience of peers, for that of adults. Don't do it to feed your ego, to tell yourself you're morally superior. Do it—invent your life, in whatever form that ends up taking, which need not be very cool or glamorous or countercultural at all—for your own sake alone.

To everything that I've been saying—about the purpose of college, the need to build a self, the value of moral independence, the virtue of confronting risk with a bold spirit—there attaches, of course, a very large qualification. You are not free to ignore reality, and the heaviest reality is money. You need to eat, and you will also need to pay for other things that college students tend to be too young to think about, especially if they've grown up in affluent families: a mortgage, if owning a house is going to be important to you (and rent, if it is not); the costs of raising children, if you plan to have them, and to send them to college in turn; a decent retirement. The Bible doesn't say that money is the root of all evil; it says that love of money is.

The economic slump, of course, has only made things harder. Jobs are scarcer, even for graduates of prestigious schools. Kids have been moving home in record numbers. The future threatens a greater degree of financial insecurity than we have had to cope with for a very long time. And then there is the ever-worsening problem of student debt. It's a lot more difficult to put aside vocational considerations and think of college as an opportunity for personal development when you know you're going to graduate with tens of thousands of dollars in loans. As one professor said to me, a family's relationship to college is going to be very different when the price is fifty thousand dollars a year than it was when it was five thousand dollars a year. If people are more apt to talk about higher education in terms of return on investment today, that's because the investment keeps on getting so much bigger.

Still, we shouldn't panic. The financial cloud is already lifting, however sluggishly, and prospects aren't likely to be as bad going forward as they've been for the last six years. Our economic mood tends to fluctuate more wildly than underlying circumstances warrant. When times are good, as anybody who recalls the pre-crash years will know, we think the party's never going to stop. When things are dark, we imagine that we'll never see the light again. There are bubbles in pessimism, too. Besides, we shouldn't kid ourselves: the utilitarian attitude that dominates our ideas about higher education, as well as the careerism that we see among elite students, did not arise as a result of the financial crash.

But we need to be brutally honest. Finding your purpose or embracing your vocation or whatever you want to call it is going to be

easier for some kids than for others. If you're lucky enough to graduate without a lot of debt, or your parents are supportive, psychologi-
cally as well as financially, you'll have a lot more room to maneuver.
The fact might shape your choice of where to go to college. Lower
cost and/or less debt might be more important, may give you more
options, than a shinier name—though it's also true that net tuition
can be cheaper (can be, not necessarily is) at a wealthier and more
prestigious school.

It isn't only about money, though. I met a student at Cornell—he
was graduating debt-free—who wanted to be a writer, but, he told
me bitterly, he wasn't even going to give it a shot, because unlike
the kids at Yale, he didn't have the necessary contacts. Never mind
the blazing misconceptions there; the point is that a sense of inner
freedom is essential. How much uncertainty you can stand (as well
as how much money you can manage on, whether in your twenties
or in later life) will depend on who you are—and although I believe
that college is an opportunity not only to discover but to reshape
who you are, there are limits to the extent to which you can do that.
Ideas can expand, values can change, but our personalities are a
great deal less elastic. Some of us are simply born with sanguine dis-
positions; for others, the glass is always half empty.

But if we're going to be brutally honest, then we need to say this
as well: all these issues are a lot easier for the kinds of kids who attend elite schools. If you go to Johns Hopkins or Bowdoin, or even
Emory or Bates, you are already very fortunate. People will hire you
more readily; graduate schools will admit you more easily. You've
been socialized into the elite, if you didn't grow up there already,
and you have indeed made contacts that can help to lubricate your
way in the world. And for all the problems with elite admissions and
the way they measure merit, you are also likely to be talented and
smart, and certainly energetic and driven. Even if you don't go to the

most prestigious college, or as prestigious a one as you could have or wanted to—even if you only might have gone to a prestigious school but opted to go elsewhere—you'll probably be just fine, no matter what you choose to do. We're still a very wealthy country by any reasonable standard, which means that you've been presented with a rare and remarkable chance, one that's far more precious than the opportunity to be rich: the opportunity not to be. To find your purpose and embrace your vocation, and still to live a decent life.

**The world is not fair,** even though it should be. The genetic lottery is not fair and never will be. Having the freedom to invent your life is a privilege. Being able to follow your passion might be the ultimate form of entitlement. But decrying these facts does not eliminate them. I recognize that what I'm saying does not apply to every student or prospective student at an elite school, still less to those at other schools. The question is, does it apply to you? If so, the fact that others are less fortunate does not let you off the hook. Quite the contrary. Whenever I am asked about these issues at campus events—"What about kids from lower-income families?" or some variation thereof—the question almost always comes from someone who appears as if he'd never had to worry about money in his life. But if you *aren't* financially constrained, if you *didn't* graduate with debt, then what is your excuse? The psychic dodge that seems to be at work is similar to what we saw with "self-indulgence." Using your privilege to pursue your dreams is spiritually suspect, but using it to enrich yourself still further is somehow authentic. If you've been blessed by Mammon, the feeling appears to be, it would be disloyal not to worship him.

As for kids who really are from lower-income families, of course the tensions are much greater, the margin for error incomparably smaller. And there are other factors, too. To be the first to go to college at all, perhaps, much less to a prestigious one; to have the chance to be the one through whom your family rises into the middle class or beyond; to be able to give your parents a comfortable retirement—such considerations put an entirely different kind of pressure on your choices. I will say only this, as others have before me: don't sell your options short. Mark Edmundson tells the following story about his father, who had barely graduated from high school:

> One night after dinner, he and I were sitting in our kitchen . . . hatching plans about the rest of my life. I was about to go off to college, a feat no one in my family had accomplished in living memory. "I think I might want to be pre-law," I told my father. . . . "Do you want to be a lawyer?" he asked. . . . "I'm not really sure," I told him, "but lawyers make pretty good money, right?"
>
> My father detonated. . . . He told me that I was going to go to college only once, and that while I was there I had better study what I wanted. He said that when rich kids went to school, they majored in the subjects that interested them, and that my younger brother Philip and I were as good as any rich kids. (We were rich kids minus the money.)

I will simply add one other thought, based on my observation of friends and students from across the economic spectrum. If you grow up with less, you are much better able to deal with having less. That is itself a kind of freedom.

Other pressures exist in immigrant families, even families, as I know first hand, that have already made it to the upper middle class. Immigrants tend to be practical people, with little patience for talk of ideals. Status matters for an extra reason: just as lower-income parents want to see their children get a toehold in the middle class, immigrants look to their offspring to solidify their family's place in America. East Asian students in particular, the "new Jews," are products, like the old ones, of a tradition that exalts academic accomplishment. Confucian culture also places special emphasis on filial piety, and immigrants tend to "live through their children" in any case.

But immigrant parents, less acculturated than their kids, have a more restricted view not only of what's out there in America—the possibilities an affluent, dynamic society affords—but even of what constitutes success in the terms they already embrace. Nothing but the Ivy League existed in my family, and much the same has been said about Asian communities today. Even schools like Williams and Amherst are off the map. I think in this connection of the story of the Exodus. The "generation of the wilderness," the ones who had escaped from slavery, were made by God to wander in the desert for the balance of their lives, barred from entrance to the Promised Land. Only their children, born into freedom, were fully equipped to make use of it.

And yet there are parents who understand what they can really give their kids. Marco Rubio, nobody's idea of a hippie, has had this to say about his mother and father: "Early on my parents drove it into us that a job is what you do to make a living; a career is when you get paid to do something that you love. They had jobs so I could have a career." The value of parental support, moral even more than financial, cannot be overstated. "Don't worry, you're young, you have your entire life," a student told me that her father said to her. "Of course you have a future. Everyone has a future. You just don't know what it's going to be yet."

But there is something that's a great deal more important than parental approval: learning to do without it. That's what it means to become an adult. A child who never rebels remains a child forever. Generational conflict was not invented in the 1960s. It is a normal part of growing up, an integral feature of human society. What isn't normal is the situation that we have today: the helicopter parents and their children who call them from college after every class—that insidious alignment of perspectives and identification of interests. What isn't normal is the notion that parents and children, first and foremost, should be "friends."

Disloyalty, says the great child psychologist D. W. Winnicott—he means disloyalty within the family—is "an essential feature of living," for "it is disloyal to everything that is not oneself if one is to be oneself. The most aggressive and therefore the most dangerous words in the languages of the world are to be found in the assertion I AM." But now it seems that families have signed a pact: never to separate, never to be disloyal. I won't grow up, and you won't make me. You won't grow up, and I won't have to face the grief of losing you. Moving back in with your parents after graduation, we need to remember, was already common before the financial collapse. If children don't rebel today, is that because they do not feel the need to—after all, we're friends!—or because they sense that it would not be safe to? Rebellion doesn't happen all at once. You need some room to test the boundaries. But if any move away is seen as a threat, the process will never begin. Better the tyrannical patriarchs of yesteryear, toward whom one openly declared one's enmity, than to have such friends as these.

"One for me, one for my parents," students will explain when you ask them why they're double-majoring in things like Spanish and economics or history and computer science. But why not simply one for me? Aren't you the one who's going to have to live your life? What do you owe your parents? Love, and when they need it later, care, but not submission. Not your life. What do you owe your parents? Nothing. The family is not a business deal. You don't "owe" your parents; you have a relationship with them. When you are still a child, that relationship ought to involve obedience. Once you're an adult, it has to involve independence. Negotiating the perilous passage from one to the other is what adolescence is about, but if you wait for your parents to make it happen, it probably never will.

So here are a few suggestions about the way you ought to conduct yourself when you go off to college. Don't talk to your parents more than once a week, or even better, once a month. Don't tell them your grades on papers or tests, or anything else about how you're doing during the term. Don't ask them for help of any kind. If they try to interfere with course selection or other aspects of your life, ask them politely to back off. If they don't, ask them impolitely. Make it clear to them that this is your experience, not theirs.

"My parents would kill me" goes the common phrase: if I majored in music, if I went on that road trip, if I took a leave of absence. So here is an idea: kill them first. No, I don't mean literally. But as Stanford professor Terry Castle put it, in an essay called "The Case for Breaking Up with Your Parents," "to live an 'adult' life, a meaningful life, it is necessary . . . to engage in a kind of symbolic self-orphaning":

> the self-conscious abrogation of one's inheritance . . . the cultivation of a willingness to defy, debunk, or just plain old disappoint one's parents, that is the absolute precondition, now more than ever, for intellectual and emotional freedom.

Of all the questions students ask me, the most common is also the hardest. It is some version of "So what should I do?": where should I go to school? what should I study? which direction should I go in afterward? Of course, these aren't the kinds of questions I or anybody else can answer, though I certainly understand the feeling of wishing that somebody could. The only concrete suggestion I can offer is one that you've already heard: Take time off. Take time off to slow down, to give yourself perspective, to break the cycle of incessant achievement, to get away from constant supervision, to see that there's a world outside of school, to develop skills and explore capacities you haven't had a chance to cultivate.

Take time off before you go to college. So-called gap year or bridge year programs are increasingly popular and increasingly encouraged. Harvard, Tufts, and NYU are now among the schools that suggest the option right in their admissions letters. Princeton has started a program of its own. Especially given the problems that more and more students are having adjusting to college, schools want kids who've had a chance to do some maturation. New programs are being started all the time, and there are websites and gap year fairs that can help you sort through them. (There are many shorter options, too, but the last thing you should do is try to cram in lots of little ones—another iteration of the hyper-distractible, resume-stuffing mentality.) Cost, of course, is an issue, but parents should consider that money spent preparing their kids to get the most *out* of college will help them to avoid wasting the money they're already planning to spend *on* college. I was prevented from doing the gap year program that all my closest friends were going on because my father was worried that it would "knock me off my path." The result was a failed college experience and a much longer detour later.

But you should also consider taking a gap year, without the "program" part. Too much structure is among the things you need to get away from—and so is the notion of being "productive." "Take a year *on*," a lot of these programs say: that is, keep enriching yourself in approved ways (go abroad and learn a language, etc.), ways that ultimately feed back into the achievement game. How about *not* enriching yourself for a change? How about doing something that you can't put on your resume (or brag about on Facebook)? How about just wandering, literally or metaphorically, or holing up and reading somewhere? How about getting a lousy apartment with a bunch of friends (or a bunch of strangers who need another room-mate) and supporting yourself with a part-time job? If nothing else, you'll probably meet the kinds of people that you'd have never had a chance to otherwise. How about practicing your moral imagina-tion by dreaming something up that no one else, including me, has thought of? If you've already gotten into school, what exactly do you have to lose?

Take time off during college. Take a leave of absence, for a se-mester or a year, when you hit the wall that Harry R. Lewis, the Harvard dean, described, and you wake up wondering what it's all been for. I can't tell you the number of students I knew who did that and returned to college strikingly different people—fuller, more in-dependent, more present in their lives, and ready to cut through not only the academic but also the social bullshit. And the way things work today, you don't even necessarily need a leave of absence. Just take a *summer* off, for heaven's sake. Don't do an internship; don't do a fellowship; don't do anything to advance your career. Just go somewhere and breathe. You'll be amazed at what you discover. Yes, you'll be "behind" those other kids, the ones who didn't "waste" their summer, but what's the purpose of being at the right point, if you're on the wrong path?

Take time off after college. Though now, of course, it's just called life. You're not taking it "off," because there is no "on" anymore, no thing that you have to return to. Graduation is the moment of maxi-mum possibility as well as of maximum freedom. There are very few opportunities that are open to you then—graduate and professional programs, for instance—that won't be available a couple of years later. I think of the Amish institution of *rumspringa*—or at least, of the image it's acquired in popular culture, as a period when young people leave their community to taste a different way of life before deciding whether to return. The upper middle class is also a kind of sect, even if the dress code isn't quite as strict, and it will still be there if you feel like going back.

**Remember that college is only** the start. "Finding yourself" means finding who you are outside of the framework of school. Extracurriculars and even summer jobs and internships are not enough, because they aren't the real thing—the stakes are limited, the conditions artificially restricted, the range of options relatively small. Deciding to invent your life is not the answer; it is the beginning of a long series of questions, ones that you can only answer in the doing. "Passion finds you, you don't find it," a friend who teaches at Lewis & Clark told the incoming freshmen. "And it finds you only after a lot of hard work, most of which you *will not* be passionate about."

Give yourself time. Your twenties, as Dustin Hoffman put it, are the "question-mark decade." While I still regret the time that I wasted in college and after, I've come to see that some form of waste, some form of wandering, was necessary and good. Waste is not waste, just as practicality is not practical, if it takes you somewhere that makes you unhappy. Out of the struggles and confusions of your postcollegiate years, unexpected new directions will arise. As the author Charles Wheelan has put it, "interesting, successful people rarely lead orderly, linear lives."

I recognize that the very plethora of choices available today is part of the difficulty many students feel in finding their direction. It's the "stem cell" problem, in my student's phrase, the idea that you can be anything. I remember that dilemma, too—the desire to remain forever on the threshold of adulthood, the grief at having to surrender your sense of limitless possibility—and I remember how I got past it: by recognizing that it wasn't finally a choice between one thing and everything, but one thing and nothing. If I didn't commit to something, I would never be anything.

By the same token, however, you needn't think in terms of choosing once and for all. You do not set an ultimate destination, or if you do, you should be prepared to alter it. You tack a course, moving from point to point in the general direction that you think you should go. You gradually find out, as you work and study and reflect, as you meet new people and discover new places, what the world has to offer (a world that's always changing, too), and what it is that's inside you to give. "It's thinking too far down the road," a high school teacher said to me, "that gets kids and parents in trouble." You don't need all the answers now; believing that you do, in fact, is part of the problem. The best advice I ever got, the thing that saved me, at the age of twenty-two, from becoming a lawyer, was this: Don't try to figure out what you want to do with the rest of your life. You're going to be a very different person in two or three years, and that person will have his own ideas. All you can really figure out is what you want to do right now.

**Inventing your life is not** about becoming an artist or activist or entrepreneur or any other particular thing. It is simply about finding your way to work that's right for you, whatever that may be. Brooklyn can be as much of a salmon run, for a certain kind of kid, as investment banking. Science and engineering have suffered as much from the pre-professional mind-set as the arts and humanities have: gifted kids becoming Wall Street quants instead of physicists or dermatologists instead of geochemists. Work that might seem uninspired to others is perfectly valid as an occupational goal, as long as it is meaningful to you. Doing what your parents want is fine, as long as you have chosen it yourself.

Inventing your life is not about believing that you can be whatever you want. That's another myth that kids are fed these days: that if you only work hard enough, there isn't anything you can't become. Yes, there is. I was never going to be a center fielder, a rock star, or a concert pianist, no matter how much I might have wanted to at various times in my life. There's such a thing as talent, too, not to mention athleticism, charisma, good looks, big brains, and everything else that you have to be born with. When Aristotle said that happiness comes from exercising your particular capacities, he meant that we each have some but not others. It's no use trying to become something that you aren't equipped for, and learning who you are means finding out, in part, what you're equipped for.

Inventing your life is not about writing your own rules. Very few of us can get away with that, especially when we're young. Work is never perfect, to put it mildly. ("Work," said my friend at Lewis & Clark, "*always* feels like work.") Every job has tedious or unfulfilling parts; every one has trade-offs that you're forced to make. Your work may be autonomous but lonely, like a writer's; or it may involve operating within a dysfunctional system, like a teacher's or a doctor's; or it may mean plugging away for years before you get any traction, like an entrepreneur's. There is sure to be anxiety, frustration, perhaps humiliation, and certainly days when you wish you had done something else. There are no guarantees that you'll do great things, or find the perfect job, or be given all the opportunities you think you deserve. Eliot's "tangled circumstance" applies to everyone. We all have to find our way in the world as it actually is, and no one's going to make it easy for you just because you're charming. But that is yet another argument for trying to do what you really love—because the lousy parts are only bearable if you're enduring them for the right reasons. Of course you're going to have to compromise. But let it be a compromise, not a capitulation. Let there be something to compromise *for*.

Finally, inventing your life is not about slacking off. You'll need to work as hard as always, at least while you're getting established, but because you'll be doing it with a sense of purpose, you'll find it more fulfilling than you could ever have imagined.

Have I mentioned that it isn't easy? It's not easy. It's never easy. Life is tragic, which means, among other things, that you can't have it all. And it's going to be bad for a while. You will wander; you will blunder; you will lose heart. You'll have to endure the pity or scorn of your peers, your parents' friends, maybe total strangers. People will wonder what happened to you—you seemed so promising in high school. You'll probably go through periods of depression, as I did more than once. You will agonize, as you have to. It's going to suck, though it will suck a good deal less if you can find a supportive community, in college or afterward, or even just a few sympathetic friends. But you can get through it. You can get past it. You can find a way to invent your life.

# Seven

## Leadership

The purpose of a college education, as everyone at least pretends to recognize, does not terminate with the individual. "Give back," our students are told. "Make a difference." "Leave the world a better place." But if there is one idea, above all, through which the concept of social responsibility is communicated at our most prestigious schools, it is "leadership." "Harvard is for leaders," goes the Cambridge cliché. When an admissions officer from Stanford visited her high school, a student told me, he explained that they were looking for applicants with "leadership potential." And so forth across the range of elite institutions. To be a high-achieving student now is to constantly be urged to think of yourself as a leader among your peers and a future leader of society. "We are preparing young men and women to become leaders and change the world for the better," said the president of Princeton at a recent commencement, as if the two ideas were self-evidently equivalent. Yet what these institutions mean by leadership is very far from anything to do with social good—very far from what they used to mean, and certainly very far from what they ought to mean.

What they mean is nothing more than getting to the top. Making partner at a major law firm, or running a department at a leading hospital, or becoming a senator or chief executive or college president. Being in charge, in other words: climbing the greasy pole of whatever hierarchy you decide to attach yourself to. Winning an impressive title, so the school can brag about you on its website. I think of the wealthy donors who always seemed to be among the honorary degree recipients at Columbia each year—CEOs, mainly, with nothing in particular to recommend them, but invariably described as "business leaders." Leadership, in this conception, is essentially devoid of content.

Students understand this, of course. The need to demonstrate that leadership potential on your college application translates to a scramble to become the head of something, anything—a team, a club, the student government—or better yet, to start something to become the head of. Never mind what you do, or what good it might do—the main thing is to get the title. You want to be a leader, don't you? I heard an anecdote about an interview at Harvard. "Harvard is for leaders," the interviewer said, "so what do you want to be the leader of?" "I don't know," the answer came back. "Something." That pretty much sums up the ethos.

If *Middlemarch* assisted us with moral courage, another book can help us see the problem—in fact, the evil—of defining leadership as getting to the top: Joseph Conrad's *Heart of Darkness*, the classic novel that became the model for *Apocalypse Now*. Captain Marlow (Martin Sheen) is simply Marlow in the book. Colonel Kurtz (Marlon Brando) is Mr. Kurtz. The novel, which was published at the turn of the twentieth century, is not about Vietnam; it is about the Belgian Congo three generations before Vietnam. Marlow—not a military officer but a merchant marine, a civilian ship's captain—is sent by the company that runs the country under charter from the Belgian crown to sail upriver, up the Congo River, to retrieve a manager who has gone mad and gone rogue, just as Colonel Kurtz does in the movie.

The novel is about imperialism and colonialism and race relations and the darkness that lies in the human heart—that much is readily understood—but it is also about bureaucracy. "The Company," after all (that's how Conrad writes it, with a capital C), is just that: a company, with rules and procedures and ranks, and people in power and people jockeying for power, just like any other bureaucracy. Just like a bank or museum, just like a school or university, just like Google or the State Department or the Brookings Institution. Just like the environment, in other words, in which today's young high achievers are likely to find themselves.

Marlow proceeds upriver by stages. First he gets to the Outer Station. Kurtz is at the Inner Station. In between is the Central Station, where we get our most extensive picture of bureaucracy in action. Here is Marlow's description of the manager there:

> He was commonplace in complexion, in features, in manners, and in voice. He was of middle size and of ordinary build. His eyes, of the usual blue, were perhaps remarkably cold [. . .] Otherwise there was only an indefinable, faint expression of his lips, something stealthy—a smile—not a smile—I remember it, but I can't explain [. . .] He was a common trader, from his youth up employed in these parts—nothing more. He was obeyed, yet he inspired neither love nor fear, nor even respect. He inspired

*uneasiness. That was it! Uneasiness. Not a definite mistrust—just uneasiness—nothing more. You have no idea how effective such a . . . a . . . faculty can be. He had no genius for organizing, for initiative, or for order even. [. . .] He had no learning, and no intelligence. His position had come to him—why? [. . .] He originated nothing, he could keep the routine going—that's all. But he was great. He was great by this little thing that it was impossible to tell what could control such a man. He never gave that secret away. Perhaps there was nothing within him. Such a suspicion made one pause.*

Note the adjectives: "commonplace," "ordinary," "usual," "common." There is nothing distinguished about this person. Around the fifteenth time I read that paragraph, I realized that it was a perfect description of the kind of person who prospers in a bureaucratic environment, because it finally struck me that it was a perfect description of a boss I used to have. She also had a smile—hers was like a shark—and she also had a gift for making you uneasy, as if you had been doing something wrong, only she wasn't going to tell you what it was. And like the manager—like so many people you encounter as you negotiate your way through bureaucratic institutions—she had no genius for organizing, for initiative, or even for creating order, no particular learning or intelligence, almost no distinguishing characteristics at all. Just the ability to keep the routine going, and beyond that, as Marlow says, her position had come to her—why?

That is the great question about bureaucracies. Why are the best people so often mired in the middle, while nonentities become the leaders? Because what gets you up the ladder isn't excellence; it is a talent for maneuvering. Kissing up to the people above you, kicking down to the people below you. Being smooth at cocktail parties, playing office politics, picking a powerful mentor and riding his coat-tails until it's time to stab him in the back. Getting along by going along. Not sticking your neck out for the sake of your principles—not *having* any principles. Neither believing in the system nor thinking to question it. Being whatever other people want you to be, so that it finally comes to seem that, like Conrad's manager, you have nothing inside you at all.

Of course our most prestigious colleges are good at training leaders. The system that they sit atop might just as well as have been designed to cultivate the necessary virtues. "What people usually mean by a leader now," Mark Edmundson remarks in reference to the way the word is thrown around on campuses today, "is someone who, in a very energetic, upbeat way, shares all the values of the people who are in charge. Leaders tend to be little adults, little grown-ups who don't challenge the big grown-ups who run the place. . . . When people say 'leaders' now, what they mean is gung ho 'followers.'" A graduate instructor I knew at Yale described the students she encountered there as "entitled mediocrities." When I used the phrase in a talk, a student asked me how the university can "be a place that trains leaders" (and note how automatic that language had become for him) "without also letting in entitled mediocrities to pay the bills?" The point, of course, is that the entitled mediocrities *are* the leaders, not a small subset of rich legacies. When a published version of the talk began to circulate online, a student later wrote, the phrase was the one "in which we recognized ourselves most immediately."

Leadership had meaning once, among America's elite. The old New England prep schools, even the Ivy League of the Gilded Age—which was also the age of students like the future presidents Roosevelt—were committed to instilling what they broadly referred to as "character." Leadership meant duty, honor, courage, toughness, graciousness, selflessness. These were aristocratic values, and they came with all the reprehensible aristocratic attitudes we're now so good at condescending to, but that doesn't make them any less commendable. Leadership had content, for those fortunate sons of the upper class; the concept made demands. It meant devotion to the benefit of others, not yourself. It called for allegiance to ideals, a commitment to the stewardship of institutions, a code of public service that was something more than a commencement after-thought. The country was being entrusted to their care, and they were expected to hand it on in better shape than they'd received it. Did many fall short? Of course. But the standard was planted, and others did not.

I don't think it occurs to the people in charge of today's elite colleges that the concept of leadership ought to have a higher meaning (or really, any meaning), and if it did, I don't think they would know what to do with the thought. As for "character," the word arises only in connection with issues like cheating or date rape, as if it signified nothing more than not doing bad things. That these institutions are the linchpin of a system that is ceaselessly engaged in forming students' characters in all the ways I talked about in the first part of this book—that is, largely for the worse—is neither noticed nor discussed.

**Instead of training** "leaders," how about training citizens? How about training thinkers—these are colleges, after all—individuals who question those in power rather than competing to become them? Better yet, how about recognizing that the best leaders *are* thinkers? I don't mean academics. I mean people who are capable of reflecting critically upon the organizations, and the society, to which they belong. Better still, who have the fortitude to try to put their criticisms into practice. People who possess what might be called resistant minds: who can ask questions instead of just answering them; who can figure out not only how to get things done, but whether they're worth doing in the first place; who can formulate new directions, for a business or an industry or a country—new ways of doing things, new ways of looking at things—instead of simply putting themselves at the front of the herd that's heading toward the cliff. For what goes for inventing your life goes equally for leadership. The crucial elements are courage and imagination. The crucial task is to create a self: something there that, when the world pushes against you, is capable of pushing back.

It takes a willingness to be unpopular, however: independent thinking does, and leadership certainly does. Yet kids today are raised not only in an atmosphere of constant affirmation, but also amid the relentless inculcation of prosocial behavior. We urge them to be team players. We teach them to be cheerful, flexible, and conciliatory, to always seek consensus and compromise. So intent have we become on avoiding painful feelings, both within ourselves and among ourselves, so committed to group harmony, so vigilant against offense, exclusion, confrontation, and other aspects of being human, that we've ended up with kids whose edges have been sanded off.

This is what you have to fight within yourself. It's not enough to resist accepted ideas; you also have to resist the people who purvey them, which is pretty much everyone: your parents, your teachers, your peers, your friends. Your group, whatever that may mean to you—an identity group, a party, a church. If you're an environmentalist, it means the other environmentalists. If you're a libertarian, it means the other libertarians. Acting with a group does not mean thinking with a group. In every context, there are questions that you aren't supposed ask. The job of a leader, the job of a thinker, is to identify and ask them. This is where courage comes in. People don't like it when you challenge the consensus, especially when it's one that's so pervasive that they do not even realize that it exists. When you question it, you're forcing them to question it as well. You're drawing out the doubts they've worked so hard to keep in check.

"The dissident impulse," says Andrew Delbanco, the "impulse to say no," has traditionally been a very powerful one in American culture. But it's hard to see much trace of it today—not even among the young, and certainly not among the young on selective campuses. Students now no longer seem to make the kind of fundamental demand upon society—that is, for a different world—that would once have been seen as a matter of course. Let me quickly add that "now," in this respect, began about forty years ago, not long before I went off to college myself. The common wisdom goes that the idealism of the 1960s was an artifact of the postwar boom, killed off by the recession of the 1970s. So why has nothing changed since then, not even during the Clinton years, a time of genuine prosperity? I was there for the anti-apartheid protests at Columbia in 1985, near the height of the Reagan recovery. "We'll get B's!" our charismatic leader reassured us (and himself) as we sat outside on our blockade. In other words, don't worry, we'll get down to studying in time for finals, and even if our grades aren't perfect, they'll still be good enough. (Today he'd say, "We'll get A-minuses!") The October Revolution this was not.

By 1987, Allan Bloom was remarking that students lacked not only a "discontent with the present," but even an awareness of alternatives. "There are none of the longings, romantic or otherwise, that used to make bourgeois society, or society in general, repugnant to the young." Bloom, a man of the right, was hardly nostalgic for the sixties. He knew, however, that rebellion as the mode of youth began not then but with modernity itself, the age of the Romantics and the American and French revolutions. To question everything, to melt down the world in thought and seek to reforge it anew, was seen, for the better part of two centuries, as the duty and privilege of being young. Great changes came of this, of which the rights revolutions were only the final chapter. The sixties were not the exception; we are.

I think of those students at Pomona, the ones who told me that they feel such pressure to be happy. A regime that seeks to stamp out feelings of unhappiness and discontent: the situation sounds dystopian. Not only is unhappiness a normal part of life—and certainly a normal part of being young—it is indispensable for any kind of transformation: of the self, of institutions, of society. Change is driven by the tension between is and ought—a tension that you have to feel inside your soul. But perhaps it's no surprise that students at selective colleges feel so little distance from the system. After all, it's working rather well for them. In his famous essay "The Organization Kid," David Brooks remarked upon "the calm acceptance of established order that prevails among elite students today." The piece was published in 2001, and while the intervening years may have troubled the calm, they've done nothing that I've seen to disrupt the acceptance.

The responses to these criticisms, when I've made them in campus talks, have tended to go like this: What about Teach For America? What about Facebook? What about the Arab Spring, not to mention Occupy? What about the whole generational effort, increasingly conspicuous, to "make a difference," typically through nonprofit or socially responsible for-profit entrepreneurship? To take the final question first: yes, things do seem to be better than they were in the 1980s and '90s. Whether due to 9/11, climate change, the financial collapse, the Internet, or a combination of them all and more, Millennials appear to be more socially engaged than any generation since the heyday of the baby boom, and to be doing some genuine good in the world. More power to them.

But that isn't the end of the story. "What about Facebook?" means "Doesn't the invention of Facebook prove that kids today, especially the kind of high achievers who attend elite universities, are changing the world for the better?" The question is symptomatic, for it betrays a confusion about the nature of social change. Facebook is only a tool. Whether it redounds, on the whole, for good or ill, is open to question and probably always will be. New technologies played a role in the Arab Spring (though one that may have been exaggerated by the Western media), but they are also playing a role, as is becoming ever more apparent, in allowing governments and corporations to surveil and control us. Tools are value-neutral. Revolutions in our tools—the kind that have been wrought by Facebook, Apple, Google, and so forth, the kind so many young people dream of making, as they work on their gadgets and apps—do not necessarily alter the structure of society, and certainly not necessarily for the better.

But how many, in today's young generation, even think of altering the structure of society, or would want to if they did? "Work within the system" is the ethos. Forget about ideals and ideologies and big ideas, those scourges of the twentieth century. Just pick a problem and go to work on it. The notion is technocratic, and bespeaks the kind of technocratic education students get today. No holistic thinking is involved, no speculation as to fundamental ends. The world, like a test, consists of a series of discrete problems, and all we need to do is get out there and solve them. Better clean technologies, improved access to drinking water, more effective schools (ace your classes, do your service projects, start a club or two): check, check, check.

Tackling such issues is both valuable and admirable. But is it enough? That system that you want to work within: what if it *is* the problem? Can we fix our schools without addressing inequality?

Can we help to lift developing countries out of poverty without reforming global trade? Can we deal with climate change by altering consumer behavior, or is the source of our environmental crisis not consumerism itself? And underneath these questions, what's our vision of the world toward which we're working in the first place? Is it just a slightly better version of the one we have today? What values are we operating from, before we get to the solutions that express them? You can banish talk of ideologies and governing ideas, but not the things themselves. The only question is whether you are conscious of your own. If not, you've probably just adopted those that happen to be fashionable now, and you almost certainly aren't aware of how they shape the way you think and act.

The spirit of do-it-yourself social engagement also goes along with a withdrawal from politics, inherently a sphere of conflict as well as of large institutions (another thing Millennials often say they can't abide). A Stanford professor told me about a couple of internships that were available to his students not long ago. One, at a small environmental nonprofit in the East Bay, drew several hundred applications. The other, at the office of the Speaker of the California State Assembly—the second-most-powerful person in the twelfth-largest economy on the planet—drew three. Not three hundred: three. I know that the idea is to begin at the edges and work your way in toward the center, but as long as there are politicians standing at the center with their arms folded, what happens at the edges will stay at the edges. We can start all the organic farms we want, but we couldn't stop Congress from declaring pizza sauce a vegetable. Local, small-scale change is great, but against the immense power of coordinated wealth—the lobbyists, the super PACs, the billionaires—the start-up model does not amount to very much. You may not be interested in politics, but politics is interested in you. Withdrawing from it doesn't make it go away.

Millennials did not invent the culture of creative, socially engaged entrepreneurship, which has been around for at least a couple of decades. So think about the way that things have changed over the last twenty years. Think about the way they've changed in terms of technology and food, the areas that that culture cares about the most. Smartphones, iPads, farmers' markets, sustainable agriculture—great, right? (Great for those who can afford them, anyway.) Now think about the way they've changed in terms of politics and economics, the things with which that culture refuses to dirty its hands. The Iraq War, *Citizens United*, the financial crisis, ever-widening inequality. That doesn't look to me like such a deal. While the "creative class" is busy playing with its toys, the world is circling the drain.

The suspicion arises that the small-scale/techie/entrepreneurial model represents the expression not of a social philosophy (especially since Millennials don't like philosophies), but of the desire for a certain kind of lifestyle. Who doesn't want to be autonomous? Who doesn't want to live somewhere cool? Who doesn't want the chance to make it big? But those are some of the things that you might have to surrender for the sake of engaging in genuine change. Politics is an ugly, incremental war, and most of those involved in it are down there in the trenches. Plenty of elite college graduates go to Washington to take up policy positions. The reason that so few attempt elective office, I was told by one of the rarities who has (he is now the mayor of a small midwestern city), is that it means going home, probably somewhere deeply unhip, and working your way up from the bottom.

I've noticed something similar when it comes to service. Why is it that people feel the need to go to places like Guatemala to do their projects of rescue or documentation, instead of Milwaukee or Arkansas? Is it because it's fun to visit poor people in other countries, but not so fun at home? When students do stay in the States, why is it that so many of them seem to head for New Orleans? Perhaps it's no surprise, when kids are trained to think of service as something they are ultimately doing for themselves—that is, for their resumes. "Do well by doing good," goes the slogan. How about just doing good? Why is that an insufficient goal? "Service" is a lot like "leadership," and in fact the two are far too tangled up. Kids want to save the world, a Brown professor told me, but their idea of doing so invariably involves some form of getting to the top.

The problem with "service" begins with the concept itself, or at least what it's become. The word is rooted in the Bible. Serve God, the Children of Israel are told, not Pharaoh. Serve God, Christ says, not Caesar. That is who you're supposed to be serving with "service." It's about humility, not condescension. But now we understand the concept in a very different way. "Giving back," "giving to others": this is the language of charity, enforcing ideas of debtorship, disempowerment, hierarchy, and social relations as economic exchange. It is us versus them, rich versus poor, white versus black and brown, the server and the served. It isn't even noblesse oblige, because there's no "oblige," no concept of obligation or social duty. "Service" is a flock of middle-class messiahs, descending in all their virtue, with a great deal of self-satisfaction, every once in a while, when they remember to think about it, upon the miserable and helpless. Like "leadership," it is a form of self-aggrandizement.

So what is the alternative? Not charity, but justice. Not "concern," but outrage. Not giving 5 percent, but changing 100 percent. Not "the superficial motions of volunteerism," as the writer and activist Tammy Kim has put it, not the palliation of social violence, but solidarity and mutual identification and working together toward a larger good that embraces us all. No wonder students prefer Guatemala to Milwaukee. Confronting injustice in your own society tends to be a lot more fraught, especially if it forces you to acknowledge the ways that you're complicit in it.

So what about Teach For America, or the Arab Spring, or Occupy? Well, what about them? Did you have anything to do with them? This is not about some moral balance sheet—society's, or Millennials', or the Ivy League's. The fact that TFA was founded by a Princeton graduate in 1991 does not let you, or Princeton, off the hook (quite apart from the fact that TFA is a sterling example of service both as resume-building and as ruling-class messianism). The Arab Spring happened on the other side of the world (and petered out, in any case, as the liberal, tech-savvy young were outmaneuvered by people who knew how to organize, and who were driven by a big idea). As for Occupy (which also doesn't look so great in retrospect), the movement was notably weak on selective campuses, where students tend to find themselves on the bright side of social inequality, and where people believe, as we know, in working within the system. Doing a little service in college, or once a year on Martin Luther King Day, does not acquit you of moral responsibility—and talking about the service that somebody else did certainly does not.

**I'm not suggesting that students** should take to the streets, or that we ought to reenact the sixties. Every person needs to find their own path, when it comes to working for a better world, and so does every generation. I'm suggesting that the first thing that you need to do—the thing that college ought to teach you to do—is think. The critic Lionel Trilling quotes the title of a colleague's essay: "The Moral Obligation to Be Intelligent." The point is not to have a high IQ. The point is to use it. Intelligence is not an aptitude. It's an activity—and an ethical activity, to boot. We don't need students to be radicals; we only need them to be skeptical. "Skeptical" comes from a word that means "to look." A skeptic is someone who bothers to look. What good does it do if you make it to the top, if by the time you get there you are just another "leader"—another opportunist, another genial conformist, another mediocrity?

When I talked about George Eliot's rebellion, I said that she believed that love was more important than a legal contract. That must have sounded pretty unremarkable. Who does not believe that now? But there's a reason that we do, and the reason is George Eliot. Not her alone, of course, but her and a few others like her—a very few, at first. There is technological progress, whose heroes are people like Edison or Jobs, and then there is social progress. The final line of *Middlemarch* is this: "that things are not so ill with you and me as they might have been, is half owing to the number who lived faithfully a hidden life, and rest in unvisited tombs." We are freer and happier (at least in certain ways) because others have come before us and were willing to run the kinds of risks George Eliot did. It is through such acts of imagination and courage that society makes its moral advances: whether they are public and collective acts, like the civil rights movement—an enormous demonstration both of imagination, the idea that things can be different, and of courage, the will to make them so—or private ones, the kind that seep into the social bloodstream and slowly change its chemistry.

Emerson insisted that we each must win our independence by mounting a private revolution to free ourselves from the tyranny of existing mental structures. Independence, revolution, tyranny, freedom: concepts that are essential to America's collective history, as well. Emerson took the national act as exemplary for the individual life. America's revolution was also an intellectual one. It also overthrew existing modes of thought, existing ideas about the way the world can look. Franklin, Adams, Paine, Jefferson, Madison: America was founded by intellectuals, by thinkers, by readers—by people who risked their lives, their fortunes, and their sacred honor in order to build a better society by speaking truth to power. Independence, impoliteness, disagreement, dissent: these values are encoded in our national genetics.

We have always seen our nation as a work in progress. We are always striving to create a more perfect union. So college is indeed about more than just you. If you are going to be the leader that your education is supposedly preparing you to become, then you need to question the very terms of that education itself. Instead of worrying so much about building your resume, you need to start working on building your mind.

# PART 3

*Schools*

# Eight

## Great Books

Creating a self, inventing a life, developing an independent mind: it all sounds rather daunting. How exactly is college supposed to help? By deploying that most powerful of instructional technologies: a liberal arts education, centered on the humanities, conducted in small classrooms by dedicated teachers. This is not a cheap or "innovative" enterprise, but it is still, and will be for the imaginable future, an indispensable one.

What are the liberal arts? They are those disciplines in which the pursuit of knowledge is conducted for its own sake. The liberal arts have nothing to do with liberalism in the political sense. "Arts" can be misleading, too, which is why the larger term is often taken to denote the humanities. But the liberal arts, in their proper definition, include the sciences and social sciences, as well. They stand in contrast to applied or vocational fields like nursing, education, business, and even law and medicine (though they furnish the knowledge that underlies them) because, as Louis Menand has put it, they are conducted "without regard to any vocational utility, any financial reward or ideological purpose." In the liberal arts, you pursue the trail of inquiry wherever it leads. Truth, not use or reward, is the only criterion.

That is why you don't just learn a certain body of material when you study the liberal arts; you learn how knowledge is created. You don't acquire information; you debate it. How do we know it is true? What further questions does it raise? What are the premises that underlie the discipline in question (be it biochemistry or political science or American studies), and what are the methods by which it proceeds? You learn, in other words, that there is no "information," strictly speaking; there are only arguments. You do the hard, slow, painstaking work—four years is scarcely adequate to make a decent start—of learning to analyze the arguments of others and to make your own in turn: to marshal evidence, evaluate existing authorities, anticipate objections, synthesize your findings within a logically coherent structure, and communicate the results with clarity and force.

The historian Simon Schama tells the story of a student who approached him after a lecture to complain that his father hadn't sent him to Harvard to become more confused. Yes, Schama answered, he did, or at least, he should have. College is the place to learn that most of what we believe (history is exemplary in this regard) is much more provisional and complicated than we usually care to admit. That may sound like mental masturbation—the pointless multiplication of complexity and nuance, the endless entertainment of theories, hypotheses, and alternatives, everything that people mean by "academic" in the pejorative sense. What it is, in fact, is an honest confrontation with reality. The world is full of immensely intricate things: the structure of an enzyme, the language of a Shakespeare play, the workings of a modern economy. Despite our urge for clear and simple answers, the truth is very hard to come by. Some knowledge is settled enough to be regarded as factual—the Laws of Thermodynamics, the dates of the French Revolution—and mastering a portion of it is a part of education, too, but the leading edge of discovery is always a blur, always a grope. We proceed by doubt, by trial and error, by resisting the impulse to lunge after certainty.

To receive a liberal arts education is to begin to appreciate this. But it is also more. Implicit in the notion of such education as it is practiced in the United States is the concept of breadth. You concentrate in one field, but you get exposure to a range of others. You don't just learn to think; you learn that there are different ways to think. You study human behavior in psychology, and then you study it in literature. You see what philosophy means by reality, and then you see what math or physics does. Your mind becomes more agile and resourceful, as well as more skeptical and rigorous. And most important of all, you learn to educate yourself.

**All of this explains why** liberal arts graduates are so highly valued in the workforce, and why it almost doesn't matter what you study. That's right: highly valued, largely regardless of major, despite what everybody seems to think. "Your College Major Is a Minor Issue, Employers Say," runs a recent headline in *The Wall Street Journal*. A survey of 318 companies found that 93 percent cite "critical thinking, communication and problem-solving skills as more important than a candidate's undergraduate major," in part because they are filling positions with "broader responsibilities" and "more complex challenges" than in the past. "There's been a big disconnect between what employers say to educators," notes Carol Geary Schneider, president of the Association of American Colleges and Universities, "and what the public and policy leaders believe matters in college."

If certain majors end up earning higher average salaries than others, the *Journal* adds, the fact has more to do with the kinds of industries those students tend to choose to enter. It's no surprise, in other words, that the pay of people who go for the bucks (economics majors, say) is higher than that of those who don't. But it's a matter of choice, not necessity—earning *desire,* so to speak, not earning potential. Part of what you learn from majoring in something that actually interests you is that there are more fulfilling ways to spend your time than trying to be rich. Starting salaries, what's more, turn out to be misleading. A recent long-term study found that while vocational majors do indeed enjoy a wage premium immediately after graduation, it all but disappears within a decade. A proper education prepares you for your whole career, not simply your initial job.

Another recent survey found that 30 percent of companies were recruiting liberal arts graduates, second only to engineering and computer science, at 34 percent, and far ahead of finance and accounting, at 18 percent. "Companies are looking for soft skills over hard skills now," said the head of the firm that conducted the study, "because hard skills can be learned, while soft skills need to be developed." And the latter seem to be in short supply. The survey cited by the *Journal* found that only 44 percent of employers believe that graduates have what it takes for any real advancement in their organizations. According to other studies, "only a quarter of college graduates have the writing and thinking skills necessary to do their jobs." Graduates are said to have trouble "communicating and working in teams, and often struggle to see complex problems from a variety of angles"—exactly the kind of vision a liberal arts education instills. "Increasingly, anything you learn is going to become obsolete within a decade," says Larry Summers, the former secretary of the Treasury and president of Harvard. "The most important kind of learning is about how to learn."

Writing in the *Harvard Business Review*—in an article titled "Want Innovative Thinking? Hire from the Humanities"—Tony Golsby-Smith, the founder of an Australian consulting firm, remarks that people "who study Shakespeare's poetry, or Cezanne's paintings, say, have learned to play with big concepts, and to apply new ways of thinking to difficult problems that can't be analyzed in conventional ways." Humanities majors, he says, are well equipped to handle complexity and ambiguity, think creatively, communicate persuasively, and understand the needs of customers and employees. "If you want another good reason to hire from the humanities," he concludes, "consider this: consulting firms like McKinsey and Bain like to hire them for all the reasons I've described above. You can hire liberal arts graduates yourself, or you can pay through the nose for a big consulting firm to hire them to do the thinking for you."

Professional schools are also awakening to the value of a liberal arts education. Medical schools, recognizing that doctors need to deal with people as well as diseases, are increasingly interested in admitting humanities and other nonscience majors. Bhaskar Chakravorti, a senior dean at Tufts University's Fletcher School of Law and Diplomacy, has written about the need for MBA programs to move away from training "super-specialists" and toward developing lateral, integrative thinkers. Engineering programs have also started to recognize the importance of giving their students a base in the liberal arts, precisely because technical information has a limited shelf life, while skills of thinking and communication last a lifetime. Humanities majors outperform biology majors on the MCAT, the medical school admissions test; social science majors on the LSAT, the law school admissions test; and business majors on the GMAT, the business school admissions test. They also have the highest average scores of all majors, by a wide margin, on the verbal and critical-writing portions of the GRE, the admissions test for graduate programs.

If anything, the liberal arts are more important now than ever, as a rapidly evolving global economy relies increasingly on creativity and innovation. If Thomas Friedman is right, if the future belongs to those who can invent new jobs and industries rather than staffing existing ones, then it belongs to people with a broad liberal arts education. In today's world of economic fluidity and instability, where the old career ladders are falling down, where even the traditional notion of what constitutes a job is up for grabs, the necessary aptitudes, writes Richard A. Greenwald, author of *The Micropreneurial Age*, include "breadth, cultural knowledge and sensitivity, flexibility," and "the ability to continually learn, grow and reinvent." Tony Wagner, author of *The Global Achievement Gap*, notes that even high-tech companies "place comparatively little value on content knowledge." David M. Rubenstein, the billionaire cofounder and co-CEO of The Carlyle Group, one of the world's largest private equity firms, put it this way earlier this year at the World Economic Forum in Davos, Switzerland: "H = MC. Humanities equals more cash." Information is freely available everywhere now; the question is whether you know what to do with it.

Even as we retreat from our traditional commitment to the liberal arts, in K–12 as well as college—"math and science" is the mantra, from our president all the way down and from kindergarten all the way up—our competitors are moving in the opposite direction. Countries like China, India, and Singapore have started to realize that the key to emulating America's creative dynamism is to go beyond the rote, technical education that they have always focused on and that we are embracing as fast as we can. The National University of Singapore has launched a liberal arts college in partnership with Yale. India's prestigious IIT's, Institutes of Technology, are moving toward a higher quotient of courses in the humanities and social sciences. Despite the strong marks their high schoolers get on international tests as well as the country's success in producing scientists and engineers, educators in China are increasingly concerned that their system isn't cultivating critical and independent minds. Some in the United States have spoken of the economic downturn, against a backdrop of continued growth in Asia, as another Sputnik moment. But after the original Sputnik, we didn't decide to emulate the Soviet Union. Apparently we don't possess that kind of confidence anymore.

All this is why the usual sneers about whether Aristotle is going to "come in handy on the job" are so utterly misguided. "After college," says a young woman who dropped out after all of a semester—she is quoted in one of those books that advise young people to forget about higher education altogether—"no one cares how well you can talk about Hume or Kant." Maybe not, but they care how well you can *talk*. They care how well you can *think*. And studying the most challenging works of art, literature, and philosophy—"being forced every day to think about the hardest things people have ever thought about," as a recent humanities graduate put it to me—is the best training you can give yourself in how to talk and think.

**Practical utility, however, is not** the ultimate purpose of a liberal arts education. Its ultimate purpose is to help you to learn to reflect in the widest and deepest sense, beyond the requirements of work and career: for the sake of citizenship, for the sake of living well with others, above all, for the sake of building a self that is strong and creative and free. That's why the humanities are central to a real college education. You don't build a self out of thin air, by gazing at your navel. You build it, in part, by encountering the ways that others have done so themselves. You build it, that is, with the help of the past. The humanities—history, philosophy, religious studies, above all, literature and the other arts—are the record of the ways that people have come to terms with being human. They address the questions that are proper to us, not as this or that kind of specialist, this or that kind of professional, but as individuals as such—the very questions we are apt to ask when we look up from our work and think about our lives. Questions of love, death, family, morality, time, truth, God, and everything else within the wide, starred universe of human experience.

The humanities are what we have, in a secular society, instead of religion. They are compatible with religion, but they have also, in important ways, supplanted it. As traditional beliefs were broken down across the eighteenth and nineteenth centuries—by modern science, by the skeptical critique of the Enlightenment—the arts emerged as the place where educated people went to contemplate those questions of meaning and value and purpose. Now the truth was multiple and personal, not settled and dogmatic. Instead of looking in the Bible, you read Dostoevsky, or listened to Beethoven, or went to see an Ibsen play. Libraries, museums, and theaters became the new churches, places where you came to court the old emotions of catharsis, transcendence, redemption, and joy. The arrangement became known as aestheticism, the religion of art. "The priest departs," said Whitman, "the divine literatus comes." *A Portrait of the Artist* dramatizes this precise transition. Instead of joining the Catholic clergy, where he would have had the power to enact the transubstantiation, Stephen chooses to devote himself to performing the miracle of literature, "transmuting the daily bread of experience into the radiant body of everlasting life"—that is, into the imperishable stuff of art.

It is no coincidence that English became an object of university study around the very time aestheticism crystallized as an idea. The center of the college curriculum slowly swung from the Greek and Latin classics, taught by rote as fixed bodies of knowledge, to English and the other humanities. (In time, religion itself was incorporated into the new system as comparative religion or religious studies. Now we teach the Bible not as scripture but as culture.) The change was actually a form of continuity. Most colleges had been founded as church-affiliated institutions; now they sought to carry on their spiritual mission under the secular dispensation. Beside the specialized programs of study in the scientific and other disciplines that were also introduced in the late nineteenth century (majors, in other words), there emerged the humanistic components of the liberal arts curriculum, including the "Great Books" and other "general education" courses that were designed to provide an opportunity for students to reflect upon "the big questions." The minister in the college chapel, preaching doctrine, gave way to the professor in the classroom, leading a discussion.

**But why art?** **What claim** does art have on the truth? If the latter is indeed so difficult to come by, then how do artists manage it? By looking very hard and long, then working very hard and long to tell us what they saw. Anyone who's tried to paint an object or a scene will understand the point. It takes tremendous concentration just to start to see what's actually in front of you, let alone to get it down on canvas: to perceive a cup of water, say, not simply as an instrument of use, something that you barely glance at as you satisfy your thirst, but in the full particularity of its material existence—the liquid color of the glass, the fingerprints around the middle, the rim of light at the meniscus, the shape of the translucent shadow that the whole thing casts.

As with painting, so with every art. In literature, what is observed is not primarily the physical world, but the psychological and social ones. The poet looks at what she really feels—about her body, or her sister—not what she's supposed to feel. The novelist reports upon the way we really treat each other—the pettiness or callousness or secret irrational longing—not the way we say we do. Those conventional modes of thought and emotion from which you need to free yourself—the party lines we spout, the happy talk that we're surrounded by—are exactly what art does its work by breaking through. There is a reason we avoid the truth, with our sociable lies and our psychological blocks: it is usually too hard to bear. "A book must be the axe," said Kafka, "for the frozen sea within us."

John Ruskin, the greatest art critic of the nineteenth century as well as one of its greatest social critics, a crucial influence on Proust, Gandhi, and many others, put the matter this way:

> *The more I think of it I find this conclusion more impressed upon me,—that the greatest thing a human soul ever does in this world is to see something, and tell what it saw in a plain way. Hundreds of people can talk for one who can think, but thousands can think for one who can see. To see clearly is poetry, prophecy, and religion,—all in one.*

Our eyes slide over the world, as we obsess about our grades or our sex life or our income. Our minds slide over it. Art, to paraphrase the poet Shelley, bursts the spirit's sleep.

To say that the humanities can be a path to truth is itself to challenge one of our most closely held beliefs. We live not only in a scientific world, but also in a scientistic one: a world that thinks that science—empirical, objective, quantifiable—is the exclusive form of knowledge, and that other modes of inquiry are valid only insofar as they approximate its methods. But the humanities and science face in opposite directions. They don't just work in different ways; they work on different things. To borrow a term from Stephen Jay Gould, one scientist who certainly understood the value of the arts, science and the humanities are "nonoverlapping magisteria," different forms of teaching that are each appropriate to their domain.

Scientific knowledge relates to external reality, to that which lies outside our minds and makes itself available for objective observation. Humanistic knowledge relates to our experience of the world, to what reality *feels* like. The painter renders the subjective experience of sight—including, especially in modern art, the dreams and dreads that we project on what we see. The novelist seeks to give us the taste of what it's like to be alive at a particular moment. I once told my brother the doctor that as a literary critic I was interested in questions of time and space. He looked at me as if I'd said that as a literary critic I was interested in performing brain surgery. But the time and space I meant were not the physicist's; they were the *experience* of time and space as represented by the novelist.

Think of time in Woolf or space in Dickens. In books like *Mrs. Dalloway* and *To the Lighthouse,* time unfolds according to the drift of consciousness, not the dictates of the clock. A sensation in the present—say, the scent of morning freshness—plunges a character back to the past. Memory, reverie, longing, a detour through a scene from thirty years ago—friends together on a terrace, half in love, with all the world before them—then a sudden jolt into the present once again, or forward to a prospect of the future. But if Woolf paints the mind as it wanders through time, Dickens gives us the experience of moving through the modern city. Broad boulevards, tight and crooked little streets, labyrinthine alleyways, mysteries of fog and shadow. We stoop to enter attics, spread our limbs in sumptuous apartments, press against the human tide at dusk. Terror, grandeur, anger, envy: the metropolitan emotions jostle up against each other as we travel through the folded urban spaces where the stranger can become a friend, identities are lost and found, and co-incidences are to be expected. No chronometer can tell us we learn from Woolf; no yardstick, from Dickens. What's wanted isn't formulas but stories.

The scientist seeks to be objective and appeals to the impersonal language of numbers. The artist speaks from individual experience and appeals to our own individual experience. Humanistic knowledge isn't verifiable, or quantifiable, or reproducible. It cannot be expressed in terms of equations or general laws. It changes from culture to culture and person to person. It is a matter not of calculation but interpretation. When we engage in humanistic inquiry—when we think about a poem or a sculpture or a piece of music—we ask, not how big is it, or how hot is it, or what does it consist of, but what does it mean. We ask of a scientific proposition, "Is it true?", but of a proposition in the humanities we ask, "Is it true *for me?*"

**Is it true for me.** Does it make sense, not to me but of me. The highest function of art, and of literature in particular, is to bring us to that knowledge of ourselves that college ought to start to give us. The ultimate reason to read the classic authors, Mark Edmundson says, "is to see if they may know you better than you know yourself." I heard from a psychiatrist who uses literature as a tool of practice ("where else does a person become aware of the subtleties of language, emotion, character, or relationships?"). Here is some of what he said:

> *I recently terminated a six-year course of treatment with a man who was initially referred because he had become addicted to narcotics. He was a deeply depressed, inhibited, bitter, and unful-filled person. I suggested that he read D. H. Lawrence, and in this*

*case, a rare exception, he took me up on the offer—the challenge
really—and for most of his treatment, Lawrence was our constant
companion. When I was a kid, people "found themselves" in literature. I found myself, for the first time when I was fourteen, in*
The Catcher in the Rye. *No more. But this man would come in
and read to me from Lawrence and say, "That's me!"*

"That's me!": the essential experience of art. We see ourselves in
the other and the other in ourselves. Freud speaks of the uncanny—
*Unheimliche* in German, un-home-like—that which is both strange
and familiar at once. So it is with the revelations of art. Art brings
us home by taking us abroad. We read of Hamlet or Jane Eyre, and
across the differences of time and place, with a pang of guilt and
bliss, we see our nature mirrored up to us, but seen as if anew. "Find
yourself" is perfect: you are reading about medieval Denmark, a
world of courtiers and princes, and all at once, as in a dream, you
somehow find yourself among them.

Art gives names to experience. We recognize Antigone or the
Wife of Bath or Madame Bovary as permanent human types—
the doomed idealist, the unabashed sensualist, the discontented
dreamer—as well as permanent potentialities within ourselves.
Think of the role that literary characters have played—Ahab, Huck
Finn, Gatsby, Holden, Sethe—in articulating the American consciousness. But art also gives you models for experience, especially
when you are young. You find in Elizabeth Bennet or Stephen Dedalus an image of the person that you want to be: Elizabeth, who turns
a snub into a laugh, who faces down the man to whom she's meant
to bend a knee, who marches at the head of all the smart and confi-
dent young women of modernity; Stephen, the artist embracing his
solitary destiny, so certain of his genius that he's willing to forsake
his family and friends. Books are maps of possible futures. They

help endow you with exactly that imagination that it takes to invent your life. The courage, too: if they can do it, so can I. Reading, says Edmundson, is "life's grand second chance." Art doesn't make you a better person; it only makes you a freer one.

But popular culture also gives you models for experience, and so does advertising. *Fifty Shades of Grey,* a Nike commercial, half the pop songs in the world: they tap directly into your id, submerging you in fantasies of pleasure. Who wouldn't want to live like that? The difference is that art provides you both the models and the means to question them. It demands that you read alertly, with your mind and not just your glands. What are the limits of living like Elizabeth? What might Stephen miss about himself? Does Holden get it wrong? Does Ahab get it right? If the liberal arts turn certainties into questions, the humanities do that, in particular, with ethical and existential certainties: our convictions about how we should act and whom we should be. Stories, says the writer Andrei Codrescu, are engines of reflection. *Middlemarch, A Portrait of the Artist, Heart of Darkness,* the *Odyssey:* literature enables us to think about our lives, just as it's been doing in this book.

Nor does that reflection only go to values. Everything we find in life we find in art. Ambition in *Macbeth* and *The Sopranos,* ennui in Chekhov and Fellini, marginality in Ralph Ellison and Arundhati Roy, and on and endlessly on. I have learned from Dante that love and hate are complements, not opposites (a good thing to know if you happen to belong to a family); from E. M. Forster, that liberal attitudes are often a cover for vanity and ignorance; from Mary Gaitskill, something of the ways the soul is manifested in the body. I don't know that any of those perceptions have influenced my choices, exactly, but they have deeply shaped my understanding of both myself and the world. Edmundson speaks of "the incessant labor of combining your own experience, taken in and metabolized by intense feeling and thought, with what you have acquired in books." Art and life, back and forth, each illuminating the other, both together creating a self.

**I said before that when** you paint an object, you have to see it in the full particularity of its existence. To borrow a phrase from Matthew Arnold, the Victorian man of letters, you have to see it "as in itself it really is." In itself and for itself—not in reference to you, as an instrument of your desire. But it isn't just things; we also tend to treat each other as extensions of ourselves. Art forces you to do the opposite. By allowing you to experience, in the most intimate and immediate way, what it feels like to be someone else—Achilles or Anna Karenina or Emily Dickinson—art instills the fundamental moral lesson: That you aren't the center of the universe. That others weren't created for your benefit. That they are just as real as you, with equal claims to dignity and understanding. "I place my faith in fiction," says the novelist and philosopher Rebecca Goldstein, "in its power to make vividly present how different the world feels to each of us." Art teaches empathy and cultivates the emotional intelligence; maybe it *can* make you a better person.

"Do you really lead a better life for having had a liberal arts education?" a student asked me once. Yes, you do, and those around you might lead better ones, as well. The social sciences are all the rage, it seems, among today's idealistic young. (David Brooks has called them "the empirical kids.") Policy, wonkery, data "Big" or otherwise: technocracy, again. But you can only measure what you know is there—and sometimes you can't measure it at all. Before you start to build a better future with "the crooked timber of humanity," as Kant referred to it, you need to find out what you're working with.

You need to know what people *are*—how they think, what they want, how they act—as well as something of the moral pitfalls of your own proposed interventions. (The law of unintended consequences is pretty much the governing principle of narrative art.) The humanities put back everything the social sciences, by way of necessary simplification, take out. Economics, for example, the most authoritative of the social sciences today, informs us that people are rational actors, forever seeking to maximize their material self-interest—an assertion that would come as news to the author of *King Lear*, let alone *The Brothers Karamazov*. Only literature, in the words of the diplomatic strategist Charles Hill, is "methodologically unbounded" enough to show how the world really works. I've heard it said that novels are obsolete, that books like *War and Peace* belong to an age when information could be delivered only in extremely inefficient forms. But *War and Peace* doesn't tell you the same kinds of things that you can learn from a blog post or a Wikipedia entry, not even fourteen hundred pages of them. It needs to be big and complex because it's telling you something that's big and complex. It doesn't give you "information"; it gives you life.

The humanities, unlike the natural and social sciences, are also historical disciplines. English is the history of English literature; religious studies is the history of religion; and so forth. And you cannot understand the world, you cannot even understand yourself, unless you understand the past, for that is largely where your thoughts and feelings come from—not to mention almost all the laws and attitudes and structures that we collectively live by. To study the past is to continually have the experience of realizing, Oh, so that's why I think that. That is what is speaking through me when I say that. The critic Northrop Frye remarked that a liberal arts education ought to lead to a recognition scene, as at the climax of a play. But in the study of the liberal arts, he said, the thing we come to recognize is ourselves.

"The most successful tyranny," said Allan Bloom, is "the one that removes the awareness of other possibilities." The past gave rise to the present, but it is also different from the present. It shows us that things do not have to be the way that they are now. It provides us with a vantage point from which to see that our conventional wisdom is just conventional, not wisdom—that what we think is natural is merely cultural; temporal, not eternal; particular, not universal. It offers us an exit from the present. It tells us that things change: not only don't they have to be the way they are, they will not be the way they are. The past, in other words, allows us to create the future. If you want to be a leader, if you want to find a new direction, then that is where you need to start.

**The defenders of the arts** and humanities tend to give the argument away before it begins. Art is solace, we're told, or diversion, or decoration—nothing more, apparently, than a form of pleasant relaxation, highbrow entertainment for the moneyed class. The arts, we hear, contribute to the economy—as if their very point were not to show us that there's more to being human than our bodies and their needs, more to a society than its commodities. When it comes to college in particular, the argument revolves around what's known as "cultural capital," the kind of social information that equips you for upward mobility. No less a figure than Stephen Greenblatt—Harvard professor, esteemed Renaissance scholar, prize-winning author—has defended the value of studying the humanities by telling us, in part, that "cultural knowledge turns out to be good for your career."

I recognize the practical importance of cultural capital and the role of college in providing it, but I doubt that it has very much to do, at this point, with the humanities. The development of Great

Books courses in the 1920s and '30s was indeed in part intended to socialize the children of immigrants, mainly Jews and Catholics from southern and eastern Europe, into the kind of culture that had only been accessible to WASPs. But any argument in that direction, whether with respect to the new immigration or to students from the lower classes, did not survive the dethroning of high culture in the 1960s and '70s. Virgil and Rousseau are not what people talk about at cocktail parties anymore, assuming that they ever were. Leonardo and Mozart no longer constitute a shared frame of reference, unless you mean Leonardo DiCaprio. Now it's HBO and NPR and REM. No one at the dinner party is going to find out whether you know anything about Montaigne, and if they did, they wouldn't care. Cultural capital now is largely transmitted from peer to peer, as the other students ape the manners of the kids who went to Exeter or Dalton, absorbing the proper tones of voice and modes of dress, the approved consumption patterns with respect to foreign travel, progressive opinion, and extra-virgin olive oil.

The humanities are all well and good, goes another argument, for the children of the privileged, who don't need to worry about earning a living. But other students, even at selective schools, should stick to the practical disciplines: engineering, computer science, economics—quantitative fields, not verbal ones. The notion echoes something Woodrow Wilson said a century ago: "We want one class of persons to have a liberal education, and we want another class . . . very much larger . . . to forego the privileges of a liberal education and fit themselves to perform specific difficult manual tasks." Substitute "technical" for "manual" and the argument is the same. It is not the proponents of a liberal arts education who are the elitists; it is those who would reserve it for a lucky few. If you think the humanities have any value, whether as a doorway to enlightenment or just as cultural capital, then they are valuable for everyone and should belong to everyone. If they are good for the poor (as Earl Shorris argued in his famous essay "On the Uses of a Liberal Education" and demonstrated in his Clemente Course in the Humanities, a program that has now been widely copied), then they are certainly good for the working-class kid at Dartmouth or the Asian kid at Duke—and, indeed, for everyone throughout the higher education system.

Is there something condescending ("imperialistic," in the current term) about suggesting that the children of immigrants ought to study English literature and the Western classics? Perhaps, but there is also something immensely powerful, and not just in personal terms. Those Jewish kids between the world wars who were socialized into Western culture went on to take possession of it. Saul Bellow, Norman Mailer, J. D. Salinger, Leonard Bernstein, and countless others, including, somewhat later, Philip Roth, Susan Sontag, Stephen Sondheim, and Woody Allen: they propelled themselves to the center of American art and thought, transforming it in their image. The best thing that could happen to our culture now is if the Asian and Latino kids did likewise. Telling them to stick to medicine or finance is just another way of keeping those communities down.

Still, it isn't my intention here to advocate for Great Books courses. I do believe that having an acquaintance with the Western classics, the Bible included, remains essential to one's education as a citizen. They are still the major portion of our mental past. Exempting students from studying them is as much of a disservice as excusing them from learning Standard Written English; it debars them from full participation. But as our outlook globalizes and our population along with it, new pasts are growing ever more relevant. We ought to know where other people come from, too, especially since those other people now increasingly are us.

These civic purposes are secondary, though. The crucial thing is to study, not the Great Books, but simply, great books. The idea is to find yourself a few of Kafka's axes; anything that has the necessary edge and heft will do. It doesn't matter who created it or when, as long as it can do some damage, as long as it inflicts that wound. The canon is irrelevant in this respect. A real reader creates her own canon, for it consists precisely of those books that she has used to create herself.

**I'm also not suggesting that** you have to be an English major. (Though it's not a bad idea. Edmundson says that when a student studies English, he majors "in becoming a person.") I'm not even suggesting that you have to be a humanities major. I'm suggesting that you take as many opportunities as possible in college to step away from whatever specialized program of study you've decided to pursue and have the kind of experience that the humanities can give you. Of course you need to specialize—now more than ever, as knowledge grows increasingly complex. You go from being a political science major to being a law student to being an attorney for the State Department to being an attorney for the State Department who focuses on issues of global trade. You study biochemistry in college, attend medical school, do a surgical residency, and end up performing kidney transplants. You major in art, get a PhD, specialize in Flemish painting, and become an expert in Van Eyck. It takes a huge amount of time. Who can afford to get a general education, too?

The mistake lies in supposing that the two objectives are antithetical—though admittedly, the notion that they are lies deep within our culture. We speak of action versus contemplation; in the Renaissance, the terms were "arms" and "arts"; in Rome, *otium* (leisure, with connotations of reflection) and *negotium* (business, like "negotiate"). But the ultimate idea of a liberal arts education is to render that distinction meaningless. There isn't life over here and work over there, general courses for the first and your major for the second. The perspectives that you get from studying the general—the wisdom, to come right out and say the word—are meant to interpenetrate the practice of your specialty.

For while it is inevitable that you will train yourself to do, at most, a small set of things, it is not inevitable that you will only think about those things. What the habit of reflection will enable you to do—what maintaining contact with art and history and philosophy (or for that matter, if you do go into the humanities, with the natural and social sciences) will enable you to do—is bring the full range of human experience, of your experience, to bear upon your work. If you become a doctor, it will make you a healer instead of a pill-pusher, someone who treats people, not diseases. If you turn out to be a professor, it will mean the difference between becoming a pedant, who teaches courses, and a mentor, who teaches students.

In fact we're suffering today from just such a cadre of technocrats, just such a specialized elite. The problem with our leaders now is not just bureaucratic cowardice; it is also a lack of ability to think outside of disciplinary boundaries. Alan Greenspan, to take the most spectacular example, has admitted that he was mistaken to assume that rational self-interest was enough to shield the bankers from disaster. As the journalist Chris Hedges pointed out, Greenspan simply couldn't see beyond his theoretical assumptions, couldn't factor in the kind of human folly to which a moment's reflection would have alerted him. Heather Wilson, a former congresswoman and longtime veteran of the Rhodes Scholarship selection process, has talked of her distress at the quality of recent applicants:

*Even from America's great liberal arts colleges, transcripts reflect an undergraduate specialization that would have been unthinkably narrow just a generation ago. As a result, high-achieving students seem less able to grapple with issues that require them to think across disciplines or reflect on difficult questions about what matters and why. . . . Our great universities . . . are producing top students who have given very little thought to matters beyond their impressive grasp of an intense area of study.*

Nor is it only our leaders. I've talked to teachers, social workers, psychiatrists, not to mention doctors, who feel that in our rush for efficiency, our addiction to methodologies and "metrics"—testing regimes, protocols, psychopharmacology, spreadsheets, the management mentality in all its incarnations—the human has been torn from what they do. The humanities are where we all can go to start to put it back.

But some professions really don't make room for anything but specialized abilities. What chance is there if you're a transplant surgeon, say, to make use of those wider perspectives? Well, you do not transplant in a vacuum. You are part of a system: a team, a hospital, a medical industry, a society. Instead of just putting your head down and doing your job, you can also look around at how things work and try to make them better. You can reflect; you can resist. You can become, in other words, a citizen. Not a leader, necessarily, but also not a follower.

This idea, after all—that school should prepare you for participation in that very rare thing in human history, collective self-government—is fundamental to our system of education. It's the reason that American schoolchildren are taught to ask questions, express their own ideas, develop their creativity, and learn by exploring and investigating. We don't teach by rote, the way they do in India.

We do not separate our ten-year-olds into academic and vocational tracks, the way they do in Germany. We don't require undergraduates to study just a single subject, the way they do in Britain. We have always wanted people who are more than merely specialists.

So what then? Are we to be a country in which everybody is dissenting all the time, challenging the way that things are done not only in the public sphere, but even in the workplace? Yes, that is exactly what we ought to be. We are a republic; we're supposed to lead together.


**In his novel** *The Marriage Plot,* Jeffrey Eugenides tells the story of a trio of students who graduate from Brown in the early 1980s. It's the heyday of semiotics. People say "what's your take?," drop the names of French theorists, score points by putting Musil on their bookshelves, and look down on classmates who imagine that literature is anything more than a bundle of "tropes." Finally, his last semester, one of the characters takes a religious studies course that affects him more powerfully than any class he's had before. It concludes with a take-home final. "You were free to consult your books," Eugenides writes. "There was no way to cheat. The answers to such questions couldn't be found anywhere. No one had formulated them yet." This is the experience that the character, Mitchell, goes through as he completes the exam (and note the way that "practical" is used):

*While he wrote, he felt, for the first time, as though he weren't in school anymore. He wasn't answering questions to get a grade on a test. He was trying to diagnose the predicament he felt himself to be in. And not just his predicament, either, but that of everyone he knew. It was an odd feeling. He kept writing the names of Heidegger and Tillich but he was thinking about himself and all his friends. . . . As he responded to the essay questions, Mitchell kept bending his answers toward their practical application. He wanted to know why he was here, and how to live. It was the perfect way to end your college career. Education had finally led Mitchell out into life.*

# Nine

## Spirit Guides

If you want a good education, you need to have good teachers. It seems ridiculous to have to say as much, but such is the state that matters have reached, both in academia and in the public conversation that surrounds it, that apparently we do. Between the long-term trend toward the use of adjuncts and other part-time faculty and the recent rush to online instruction, we seem to be deciding that we can do without teachers in college altogether, at least in any meaningful sense. But the kind of learning that college is for is simply not possible without them.

Teaching is not an engineering problem. It isn't a question of transferring a certain quantity of information from one brain to another. "Educate" means "lead forth." A teacher's job is to lead forth the powers that lie asleep within her students. A teacher awakens; a teacher inspires. We're all familiar with the way this feels, because we've all had someone who has played this role for us. A teacher is a midwife, Socrates said. If you are "pregnant in soul," he says in Plato's *Symposium*, your teacher's presence makes you teem with thoughts that beg to be released into the world. The imagery seems contradictory: are you pregnant already, or does your teacher's presence make you so? Both: a teacher helps you to discover things inside you that you didn't know were there.

But we needn't even talk about the soul. Let's stick to the mind in the narrower sense, the organ that we all agree a college education ought to go to work upon. To put it in the language of computers, you can download all the data you want, but it won't be any good to you unless you have the software to make use of it. That software, the ability to operate on information—to understand it, to synthesize it into new combinations, to discover and create with it—is what college is meant to "install." But here the analogy breaks down, for unlike actual software, the installation isn't quick and easy, and it certainly isn't passive.

Thinking is a skill—or rather, a large and complex set of skills. In terms of what they take to learn, they aren't any different than manual ones—than hitting a ball or throwing a pot. You do not learn them from a book or video or website. You learn them directly from another person. You learn them through incessant repetition and incremental variation and extension under the close supervision of an experienced practitioner. You learn them in classes that are small enough to allow for individual attention, supplemented by one-on-one instruction tailored to your own specific aptitudes and needs. If you're learning how to play guitar, the teacher will place your hands exactly where they need to go (and do it again and again until you get it right). The mind has "hands," as well, and an endless variety of things you can do with them.

Remember that the central intellectual ability that you're supposed to develop in college is that of analyzing other people's arguments and formulating your own. If mastering a skill requires ten thousand hours of practice, it's no wonder that college is only a start, with more work to do in graduate school or on the job. (You'd need to be at it for fifty hours a week, fifty weeks a year, to fit it all in as an undergraduate.) And that assumes that you receive the proper instruction. You write a paper that makes an argument. Your teacher goes through it point by point, identifying errors in logic, faults in structure, problems with the way you handled evidence, opportunities you missed, and places where objections should have been anticipated. He also raises further questions, suggests additional lines of inquiry, and commends the ways in which you did things right. Then you do it again, and again, and again, in class after class after class, slowly strengthening your skills. You write a three-page essay (that you get, at best, a C on) your first week of freshman composition, a bunch of fifteen-page seminar papers junior year, and a fifty-page thesis that you hand in a few weeks before you graduate. Or if you're a science major, you go through an analogous process with lab reports or computer programs or mathematical proofs.

In class, you do not spend your time transcribing information. The proponents of distance learning are not incorrect to believe that lectures are usually an inferior form of instruction. That is why a significant portion of classes, at least, should be small enough to run as seminars. The purpose of a seminar is to enable your professor to model and shape the mental skills she's trying to instill. She conducts a discussion about the material, but she doesn't simply let you talk. She keeps the conversation focused. She challenges assertions, poses follow-up questions, forces students to elaborate their one-word answers or clarify their vague ones. She draws out the timid and humbles (gently) the self-assured. She welcomes and encourages, but she also guides and pushes. She isn't there to "answer questions," at least not for the most part; she's there to ask them.

Some of those questions should be ones she doesn't know the answer to herself. Discussion in a seminar should be collaborative and open-ended, alive with serendipity and the energy of imminent discovery—a model, too, of how to think *together*. A student at Pomona praised his professors to me for granting students the "necessary illusion of discussing a book as a peer." Yet it isn't altogether an illusion. One of the rewards of being a professor is the chance to learn from fresh young minds as well as teach them. In *The Marriage Plot,* the class that changes Mitchell's life concerns the fate of Christianity in modern culture, whether belief remains a viable option. "Richter asked the students questions and listened to their answers as if it might happen here today: in Room 112 of Richardson Hall, Dee Michaels, who played the Marilyn Monroe part in a campus production of *Bus Stop,* might throw a rope ladder across the void." I myself became a decent teacher only when I started to relinquish some control over the classroom—stopped worrying so much about "getting my points across" and recognized that those moments of disorder that would sometimes occur, those spontaneous outbreaks of intelligence, were the most interesting parts of the class, for both my students and myself. We were going somewhere new, and we were going there together.

College teaching, like any other kind, is a slow, painstaking, difficult process. (It is also, when properly done and adequately supported, an intensely gratifying one.) It is itself a complex craft that can't be scaled or automated. You have to get to know your students as individuals—get to know their minds, I mean—and you have to believe completely, as a fellow student wrote about my own professor, Karl Kroeber, in each one's absolute uniqueness. (It was Karl who said that a genuine teacher teaches students, not courses.) "Mitchell observed Richter's thoroughness," Eugenides writes, "his compassionate revelation of error, his undimmed enthusiasm for presiding over the uncluttering of the twenty or so minds gathered around the seminar table."

My years in the classroom, as well as my conversations with young people about their college experience, have convinced me there are two things, above all, that students want from their professors. Not, as people commonly believe, to entertain them in class and hand out easy A's. That's what they retreat to, once they see that nothing better is on offer. What they really want is that their teachers challenge them and that they care about them. They don't want fun and games; they want the real thing.

**What they want, in other** words, is mentorship. I remember just how starved I was for that myself in college. I saw how starved my students were: for validation, for connection—for (let's not be shy of saying it) parental figures other than their parents. Not only is there nothing wrong with that desire, it is a necessary part of growing up. Other cultures—Jewish, Indian, East Asian—with their veneration of the teacher, recognize as much. In South Korea, so I'm told, parents warn their children that if they don't stop misbehaving, they'll tell their teachers. But in America, we're not so sure. We are possessive of our kids, jealous of other influences upon them. But in *The Path to Purpose,* William Damon talks about the critical importance of outside adults in helping young people find their way. And Mark Edmundson remarks, while acknowledging the inevitable sadness for the parents who are left behind, that "it almost seems the natural order of things that children will leave their families and strive to put themselves under the influence of other guides . . . more attuned to their rising hopes."

I heard a colleague give a presentation once on how to keep your office hour meetings under seven minutes. Sessions should be focused around specific issues; students should know why they're coming in. So far, so good: instructors certainly need to manage their time. But then she said, "Anything beside their work, I don't talk to them about. I don't offer psychological advice for the same reason that I wouldn't let a therapist grade their papers."

It was a clever line, but it bespoke a common misconception about the kind of guidance that a mentor gives. You do not talk to your students; you listen to them. You do not tell them what to do; you help them hear what they themselves are saying. You ask the kinds of questions that Lara Galinsky talks about as being important at times of decision—those "why" questions that help people connect with what they care about. Most advisors just tell you what courses to take, a student at Brown remarked to me, but the best ones "help you to think in a different way about the choice." As Harry R. Lewis suggests, a mentor looks for the questions behind the questions their advisees ask. "The most important job of the advisor," he writes, "is to help students understand themselves, to face and take responsibility for their decisions, and to support and to free them to make choices that are at odds with the expectations others have for them." Students look to mentors—figures "more attuned to their rising hopes"—to give them what their parents won't or can't: the permission to go their own way and the reassurance that their path is valid.

Lewis speaks of professors in their formal roles as academic advisors, but regardless of whose office they're supposed to go to, students gravitate toward teachers with whom they have forged a connection. Learning is an emotional experience, and mentorship is rooted in the intimacy of intellectual exchange. Something important passes between you, something almost sacred. Socrates remarks that the bond between a teacher and a student lasts a lifetime, even once the two have parted company. And so indeed it is. Student follows student, and professors know that even those with whom they're closest now will soon decline to names in an address book, then at last just distant memories. But the feelings that we have for the teachers or the students who have meant the most to us, like those for long-lost friends, can never go away. They are part of us, and the briefest thought revives them, and we know that in some heaven we will meet again.

**For all the skill that** teaching involves, you ultimately only have a single tool: your entire life as you have lived it up until the moment you walk into class. "The teacher, that professional amateur," said the critic Leslie Fiedler, "teaches not so much his subject as himself." He provides a model, he went on, "of one in whom what seemed dead, mere print on the page, becomes living, a way of life." I developed a rule of thumb in graduate school. If a professor didn't mention something personal at least a single time—a reference to a child, an anecdote about a colleague—then it was a pretty good bet that I had nothing to learn from him. It's not that I needed my teachers to be confessional; I just needed them to be *present*. "Mortimer Adler had much to tell us about Aristotle's *Ethics*," Saul Bellow wrote about the University of Chicago eminence, "but I had only to look at him to see that he had nothing useful to offer on the conduct of life."

Students want you to be honest, not least about yourself. They want you to *be* yourself. You need to step outside the role a bit, regard it with a little irony, if only to acknowledge the dissonance between the institution and the spirit. It often feels that there are certain things you cannot say inside a classroom—the most serious things that you want to say, the most genuine things. You want to say that life is tragic, that we are dangling above a void, that what's at stake, when you read a book, is nothing less than life itself. But you feel your institutional surroundings holding you as if between quotation marks. You fear that your words will fall to the ground with an audible clink. That is where a little distance from the situation is of service. Just because I say this stuff in class, I used to tell my students, doesn't mean I don't believe it.

There are two things that kids invariably tell you about their favorite professors. The first one is "she teaches about everything." That's never literally true, of course, so what does it actually mean? Great teachers, as Andrew Hacker and Claudia Dreifus remark, are not bound by disciplinary ideas of what they're allowed to say. They connect the material at hand, in a way that feels spacious and free, with anything to which it might be relevant. They connect it to experience, and so they shed light on experience—on your experience. Just as great art gives you the feeling of being about "life"—about all of it at once—so does great teaching. The boundaries come down, and somehow you are thinking about yourself and the world at the same time, thinking and feeling at the same time, and instead of seeing things as separate parts, you see them as a whole. It doesn't matter what the subject is. A student put it to me this way, about a professor in an oceanic studies program: "He made marine ecology reflect universal truths."

You know great teaching the moment you encounter it. Yes, you feel, this is it—this is what I came for. It reaches deep inside you. It satisfies desires that you didn't know you had. It makes the world feel newly large and meaningful—exactly, again, like art. The other thing that students say about their favorite teachers is "he changed my life."

**There is only one problem** with telling students to seek out good teaching in college. They're going to have some trouble finding it, because academic institutions usually don't care about it. Oh, they'll tell you otherwise, in their promotional material. But I advise you to be skeptical. The profession's whole incentive structure is biased against teaching, and the more prestigious the school, the stronger the bias is likely to be.

The trouble goes back to the conflict between the missions of the college and the university. Ever since the research model took root in the late nineteenth century, scholarship has been the path to status for both professors and schools, and teaching has been valued less and less. Already by the start of the twentieth century, Andrew Delbanco reports, "ambitious academics regarded teaching undergraduates as a distraction and a burden." The transformation wasn't instantaneous, of course. In 1923, the dean of the graduate school at Brown was warning about a professoriate that was still too committed to instruction. But he'd find little to concern him now. With the postwar, and even more, post-Sputnik explosion of funding, the research model began to diffuse itself throughout the system as a whole. "The research professor," writes Louis Menand, became "the type of the professor generally." Between 1960 and 1990, federal research funding quadrupled while average teaching hours fell by half. Publish or perish: professors' loyalties lay with their disciplines now, not with their institutions. Their validation and advancement came from research, not teaching. Their attention was absorbed by peers, graduate students, conferences, scholarly journals, professional organizations—everything except their undergraduates.

The glut of PhDs that started in the 1970s enabled schools to ratchet up their expectations. Now you had to publish more and more, whether or not the work was any good. Academic journals proliferated, as did university presses. More recently, the emergence of technology transfer as a major academic revenue stream—licensing the results of scientific discovery to private enterprise—has tilted the balance of institutional interests ever more decisively in favor of research (as well as against the humanities). Star professors, who can pull in outside funding, are increasingly coveted, and a common strategy for luring them has been to excuse them from all but the most nominal pedagogical responsibilities (as anyone who's been to Harvard knows).

But everybody wants to be a star—and every institution wants to be a player. Second-level public universities (which usually means the ones with "State" in their name, like Michigan State) now aspire to compete with their respective flagship schools (like the University of Michigan). *U.S. News* has also had its baleful role to play. Fifteen percent of an institution's score on the all-important rankings consists of "academic reputation" as judged by administrators at other schools—a measure that invariably reflects perceptions about research rather than teaching, since nobody really knows what's going on in other people's classrooms (or even, indeed, their own). "To a disturbing extent," Jennifer Washburn writes in *University Inc.*, "administrators have simply concluded that they need not concern themselves with the quality of undergraduate instruction."

How much of all this scholarship is worth a damn is open to question, but there's no debate about the impact that the focus on it has on what transpires in the classroom. "A superior faculty," wrote Clark Kerr, the architect of California's public higher education system, "results in an inferior concern for undergraduate teaching." Teaching well takes time. Challenging your students takes time: you have to assign a lot of work, and you have to comment on it carefully. Caring about your students takes time: you need to be willing to talk to them, if only about their work, and often for a lot longer than seven minutes. Just learning how to run a class takes time: how to lead a discussion, how to ask a good question, how to deliver a lecture that is worth your students' attention. The ten-thousand-hour rule applies here, too.

But every minute spent on teaching is a minute that is not devoted to research. Good teaching isn't simply undervalued; especially at elite universities, it is actively discouraged, because it's seen as raising doubts about your seriousness as a scholar. "Winning the campus teaching award," said Ernest Boyer, vice president of the Carnegie Foundation for the Advancement of Teaching, "is the kiss of death when it comes to tenure." This is not a joke. I was told by a professor at a leading university that when he was given such an honor as a junior faculty member, the provost leaned over at the ceremony and whispered, "Don't worry, this is really a good thing." Being an awful teacher, the professor later concluded, can hurt you at tenure time, but being a really good one can generate suspicion. The sweet spot, he decided, is to be unremarkable. (How's that for a slogan to put on a website? "Our teachers are unremarkable!") There is always that moment of lost innocence among undergraduates at elite schools, usually when a popular teacher is turned down for tenure, when they realize the university isn't really about them.

The unspoken premise among institutions—or at least, the unspoken rationalization—is that the best scholars make the best instructors. But there is little reason to believe as much, and a lot of reason to believe the opposite. Never mind the issue of time. Academic training actively deprives you of the qualities that make for good teaching. A good teacher speaks plainly, in vivid, accessible language, because she is addressing what amounts to a general audience. But the kind of jargon academics learn to use is designed to repel the uninitiated. A good teacher ranges widely, making connections among subjects as well as from learning to life. But academics are constrained to specialize, and increasingly, to hyperspecialize, looking neither left nor right as they plow their little corner of the field. (I asked a colleague once if he had seen a certain piece in the *New Yorker*. "No," he replied, "I don't read the popular press.") A good teacher, as I said, is personal. But academics learn to abstract themselves from the way they communicate, since scholarship is meant to be objective. Academic prose has been described as "author-evacuated," and there are classrooms one could equally describe as teacher-evacuated.

There are certainly many now that are professor-evacuated. I don't need to dwell on the shift, since the 1970s, from tenure-track faculty to contingent academic labor—adjuncts, postdocs, graduate students, and full-time non-tenure-track instructors—except to say that it's getting worse all the time. As of 2011, tenure-track professors— the "normal" kind of academic appointment—represented less than 25 percent of the American faculty. Contingent labor is a lot cheaper, never mind what its employment does to instructional quality. Adjuncts are often remarkably industrious and dedicated, especially given the fact that their pay is ludicrously low (in the vicinity, on average, of three thousand dollars a course), but they tend to be overworked, overwhelmed, and relatively inexperienced, not to mention transient. Contingent instructors also tend to cluster in the kinds of introductory courses that professors shun—the very classes where it's most important to make students feel enfranchised, as they enter the alien world of college. And when a professor *is* at the front of the room, it's apt to be a lecture hall, with actual student contact handled by teaching assistants—or at many places, simply nonexistent.

Kids know they're being cheated. One of my students told me that she had very few professors with whom she felt that she was "getting taller intellectually." Others said that one-to-one interaction with teachers was hard to come by, and real intellectual dialogue almost impossible—this despite the fact that Yale has a student-faculty ratio of 6:1, among the very lowest in the country. And Yale, it seems, is one of the best when it comes to instruction, at least among elite universities. A colleague who had taught at Harvard was amazed to find that we talked about teaching at all. A student at Northwestern told me that the kids there have to compete for their teachers' attention. A 2005 survey of college freshmen found that less than one in six were "very satisfied" with the teaching they'd experienced. A survey of seniors found that more than a third reported being "frequently bored in class."

And now, of course, come the MOOCs, those massive open online courses. Why anybody sees them as an answer is a mystery to me. Yes, they are cheaper, but they also make what's bad about the current situation even worse. Students complain that their professors are remote, so we're going to make them more remote (literally so, in fact). They feel that they have little contact with their teachers, so we won't allow them any. They need challenging assignments and detailed, individualized feedback, so we're going to give them multiple-choice quizzes that we grade by machine. Online instruction isn't just conducted on the Web; it embodies an idea of knowledge that's been shaped by the Web—by Google, by Wikipedia—a confusion of information with understanding. I still don't get why a MOOC is substantially more than a sexy textbook, one that promotes a range of practices and behaviors that higher education ought to fight against: passive learning, diminished attention, the displacement of reading by watching, teaching as showmanship, and the professorial star system. Replacing traditional courses with MOOCs would be like taking children away from a neglectful mother and handing them over to a wire monkey.

MOOCs are not about democratizing education. That is just their cover story. They're about reinforcing existing hierarchies—

and monetizing institutional prestige—as the higher education market lurches and heaves. The kids at Harvard get to interact with their professors. The kids at San Jose State get to watch the kids at Harvard interact with their professors. San Jose looks worse than before; Harvard looks even better. That is why Coursera and the rest are working with places like Princeton and Berkeley, even though their faculty are hardly likely to represent the best available, since teaching isn't why they have their jobs. The currency the MOOCs are dealing in—and from the schools' point of view, at least, seeking to maximize the value of—is not instructional quality, but prestige.

You'll know those institutions take their online courses seriously as a form of education when they start awarding credit for them. But don't hold your breath. They have no intention of diluting their brands. Kids at Dartmouth or Columbia are still going to get, and their parents are still going to pay for, the deluxe residential experience: contact (at least nominal) with famous professors, state-of-the-art facilities, endless extracurricular opportunities, and above all, the chance to meet, mix with, and marry their equally privileged or soon-to-be-privileged peers. Even in purely instructional terms, no one has claimed that MOOCs are anything close to traditional college classes. It's long been established that quality online instruction, including "blended" courses that combine the old and new modalities, is no less costly than the face-to-face variety, precisely because it is equally labor-intensive.

When the purveyors of MOOCs—or their useful idiots in the media, who usually have no experience as teachers—extol the civic virtues of their enterprise, they want us to envision that mythic child in darkest Africa who, having somehow gotten access to a high-speed connection, enjoys educational parity with every other kid in the world. In fact, that's not their target audience at all.

Coursera et al. are for-profit companies, and the universities with whom they work (and this goes for edX, the leading nonprofit, as well) expect to see a return on their considerable investment. The goal is to generate revenue, especially by licensing courses to schools that are lower on the food chain. Now that the state legislature in California—where the leading for-profits are headquartered, and where the tech business wields a lot of political clout—has pushed through a law requiring the Cal State system to accept MOOCs for credit, that objective is in sight. What we are seeing, in other words, is nothing less than the monetization and privatization of public higher education.

People like to say these days that college is a bubble, but the real bubble is the MOOCs. (In fact, Sebastian Thrun, cofounder of Udacity, has already run the flag down the pole, announcing that early experiments were a failure and that he was turning his attention to corporate clients.) Despite the recent rush in their direction, MOOCs have yet to demonstrate much benefit at all, even on their own terms. Only about 4 percent of students who start one actually finish it, but most of those are adult learners who already have degrees and are looking for enrichment or new skills—people, that is, who are capable of directing their own education. Yet that is exactly what kids go to college to learn how to do. When businesses start to hire people with online "completion certificates" rather than traditional degrees—and hire them for jobs that require complex skills and promise real advancement—we'll know that MOOCs have even the barest of practical value.

I just hope it's not too late by then. There are people out there who are looking for the chance to dismantle higher education and sell it for parts. Once that's done, it can't be undone. College is not like cable television, another service people talk about "unbundling." You can get as much out of Comedy Central whether or not you're also buying Hallmark, or out of *The Daily Show* whether or not you're also buying *The Colbert Report*, but college is a holistic, sequential, immersive experience. Institutions ought to keep in mind that the one product they have to offer that no one can duplicate or automate is, precisely, the liberal arts education.

**The only genuine solution to** the crisis in the classroom is for colleges to bring back teaching to the center of their mission. That means finding the will—and yes, the money—to reverse the long-term trends that have given rise to the present disaster: the move to contingent labor and the exclusive embrace of the research model. Universities need to staff their courses with real professors again, not academic lettuce-pickers. If we want people to do the hard, highly skilled work of educating the next generation—of workers, of thinkers, of citizens, of leaders—then we need to pay them well and treat them with respect. It isn't that professors do not make enough; it's that there aren't enough professors. Doubling the current number wouldn't overshoot the mark, and by making the academic job market into something other than the slaughterhouse it's been for as long as anyone remembers, we would also enable a larger number of our brightest students to regard the profession as a viable career path again.

But we also need to redefine the job. Very simply, more teaching, less research. We can improve pedagogical training, especially in graduate school, as some have suggested. We can offer bonus pay to those who excel in the classroom, as has also been proposed. But nothing's really going to change until we alter the basic incentives. That means one or both of two things: raising teaching to equal importance with research when it comes to making decisions about hiring, retention, promotion, and tenure, or creating a parallel teaching faculty of equal pay, job security, and institutional respect. If people could advance up the ladder through teaching or research or a combination of the two, we'd get a lot less pointless scholarship and a lot more quality instruction.

A lot of faculty would welcome this arrangement, I believe. For every egotist who thinks his monograph is going to change the world, there are probably several professors who'd be happy to surrender the grind of publication and the pretense of originality: who have long felt that they "don't have anything to say" (a phrase one often hears), who are tired of spewing jargon for the benefit of half a dozen fellow subsubspecialists, who'd be delighted to trade the often stultifying work of the library or the lab for live contact with actual students.

You want your teachers to be very smart, and you want them to know what they're talking about, but neither requires them to be leading scholars (still less, nonleading ones). Among the people I knew at Yale, the best teachers—as well as the most interesting individuals to talk to—were often to be found among the cadre of longtime instructors who helped to staff the introductory English courses. The truth is we already have a teaching faculty—those very same contingent workers. We just need to make them into a real faculty, not a class of academic helots.

There is a large, public debate in this country about primary and secondary education. There is now another, equally public debate about higher education. What I fail to understand is why they aren't the same debate. We all know that students in elementary and high school learn best in small classrooms with the individualized attention of motivated teachers. It is the same in college. Kids don't suddenly turn into different people—fully independent and intellectually self-sufficient, needing only to be plugged into a computer—the moment that they turn eighteen. Teaching isn't information transfer, and it isn't entertainment, either. It's about the kind of interchange and incitement that can only happen in a seminar—"seminar" being a fancy name for what every class already is from K–12. It is labor-intensive; it is face-to-face; it is one-at-a-time. We can try to do it on the cheap, but we will get exactly what we pay for.

# Ten

## Your Guide to the Rankings

I recently heard from a high school student who was trying to decide between Harvard, Stanford, and Yale. Could I give him some advice? I don't know, I asked him, do you think you look better in crimson, cardinal, or royal blue? That's about the only difference I can see between those places. The students, the teachers, the mentality, the madness: at those and other top-tier universities, they're all essentially the same. The rest is marketing and ego, the sorts of things psychologists have in mind when they talk about "the narcissism of small differences"—the meaningless distinctions people make to feel superior to those who are exactly like them. The real question is whether you want to continue to participate in the system that these institutions form the apex of, and if you don't—if you want to get the kind of education I've been talking about—then what are the alternatives.

I am under no illusion that it doesn't matter where you go to college. We mustn't be naïve or sentimental about this. The notion that you can get an equally good education at Fresno State as at Stanford, as the historian Victor Davis Hanson, who has held positions at both institutions, has claimed, or at Linfield College as at Swarthmore, as Hacker and Dreifus insist, strikes me in both cases as a species of willful anti-elitism. Hanson claims himself that the only difference is the students, but even if that's really true (which I seriously doubt), that's quite a big difference indeed. The students determine the level of classroom discussion and of instruction generally. They're the people you spend almost all of your time interacting with when you're not in class. They shape your values and expectations, for good and ill ("it's hard to build your soul when everyone around you is trying to sell theirs"). In fact, it's partly because of the students that I'd warn kids away from the Ivies and their peers.

But there are many options between Fresno State, which is part of the chronically underresourced Cal State system, or Linfield College, where the lion's share of students, as at Fresno, choose vocational majors, and Stanford or Swarthmore. A lot of students and families are opting to spend less on college and save their tuition dollars for graduate school, and despite relentless cuts in funding, there are still some very good public universities in every region of the country. The education is often impersonal, especially in the first two years, but the student body is usually far more diverse—genuinely diverse, diverse in terms of socioeconomic background—with all of the invaluable experiential learning that implies. A former student, now a graduate instructor at UCLA, had this to report:

> I am not someone who touts "diversity" for its own sake neces-
> sarily, but the way it arises in classes here speaks to the value
> of being in a public institution. In one of my seminars, the fact
> that one girl was Pakistani, one was Bengali, one was black and
> wheelchair-bound, and one was Israeli had an enormous impact

*on our discussion of Orientalism. You can't get away with con-*
*venient abstractions and pat analyses of the "other" under such*
*circumstances.*

There are also other benefits of going to a public university, ones that tend to be invisible to the values of the upper middle class. Here is what Brian Johnsrud, an alumnus of Montana State University and former Rhodes Scholar, now a doctoral student at Stanford, had to say:

*Two weeks ago I had the privilege to be a keynote speaker at my*
*alma mater during Career Week. If my talk had had a title, it*
*would have been "The Advantages of a State-School Education."*
*I talked about the skill set that MSU provides that you don't get*
*at an elite institution, including accountability, being forced to*
*try your best because you aren't constantly patted on the back,*
*and integrating studies with life skills like living and working*
*off campus and generally learning to be an adult.*

State schools also offer talented students a greater chance to stand out from the pack and therefore make connections with professors. "What's more," my correspondent went on,

*as I've mentored MSU students applying for scholarships like*
*the Rhodes and Marshall, I've been astounded by the incredi-*
*ble stories in their letters of recommendation. They illustrate*
*remarkably personal, engaged, and academically rigorous rela-*
*tionships between undergraduates and professors, very different*
*from Oxford and Stanford.*

Most important, for smart and motivated kids, a lot of public campuses have honors colleges or programs that provide a liberal arts education at the cost of a state institution. But public universities are not the only alternative to Harvard and its ilk. If you want a liberal arts education, the best place to look is a liberal arts college. Such institutions have potential drawbacks: they're small, which is not for everyone, and they're often fairly isolated, which is also not for everyone. They can be a little insular, a little given to self-righteousness. But if there is anywhere that teaching and the humanities are still accorded pride of place—anywhere that college is still college—it is there.

Professors at liberal arts colleges devote a larger portion of their time to teaching, are more likely to be hired and promoted at least in part because of it, and are expected to make themselves available to students and to play an active role in campus life. Although they've been socialized into the same professional system as faculty at other places, their institutional identification is also likely to be greater. Instruction at liberal arts colleges is almost entirely seminar-based, and you can be reasonably certain that there will be an actual professor at the table. There are few adjuncts at liberal arts colleges, and with no layer of graduate students between you and your professors and no large university for everybody to get lost in, the pedagogical environment is intimate and intense. (The absence of a big-time research infrastructure also means that the humanities are more than just an annex to the sciences.) Students have told me about having "nowhere to hide" in class, as well as about the long discussions they have had with their professors outside of class. They also frequently get input into matters of real consequence, like admissions, the design of new dorms, and even faculty hiring—something that's unthinkable at a research university. Liberal arts colleges are still apt to treat their students like members of a community, not just clients or customers.

But the most important difference, as always, is the kids themselves. One correspondent told me that she'd always just assumed that universities are for careerists, liberal arts colleges for people who are genuinely interested in ideas, and that seems about right. Still, we shouldn't draw too sharp a line. The way that some Pomona students put it to me was that the consulting rat race doesn't start there until senior year—as opposed to a year or two earlier, from what they could tell from their friends at the Ivies. As *U.S. News* has tightened its grip and the admissions process has homogenized the experience of high-achieving kids across the country, the most prestigious liberal arts colleges—or at least, their students—have grown increasingly similar to their Ivy League counterparts. Economics, as I mentioned, is now the most popular major at at least six and as many as fourteen of the top twenty liberal arts colleges, including seven of the top nine. (The information is provided in the back of *U.S. News.*) You ought to consider avoiding such schools.

The best option of all may be the second-tier—not second-rate—liberal arts colleges, places like Reed, Kenyon, Wesleyan, Sewanee, Mount Holyoke, and quite a few others: schools that, instead of trying to compete with Harvard and Yale, have retained their allegiance to real educational values. Look at alternative lists like Colleges That Change Lives, Hidden Ivies, or the *Washington Monthly* College Guide and Rankings, which measures institutions by their commitment to social good. Look for a school that's going to care about you, not the new MBA program in the Gulf. Be skeptical of places that tout curricular flexibility rather than intellectual rigor, or that are gutting the arts and humanities in favor of "practical" programs. Keep in mind that with the long-term glut of PhDs, there are brilliant professors everywhere now.

I also spoke about the kid who can't be bothered to get A's in every class in high school because they're actually more interested in following their curiosity, so here's another rule of thumb. *U.S. News* supplies the percentage of freshmen at each college who finished in the highest 10 percent of their high school class. Among the top twenty universities, the number is usually above 90 percent, a threshold that is also reached at several of the top colleges. I'd be wary of schools like that (though I would make an exception for public universities, which draw from disadvantaged high schools from across their respective states). Not every ten-percenter is an excellent sheep, but a sufficient number are for you to think very carefully before deciding to surround yourself with them. Kids at less prestigious schools are apt to be more interesting, more curious, more open, more appreciative of what they're getting, and far less entitled and competitive. They tend to act like peers instead of rivals.

A recent graduate had this to say about her college experience:

> *I remember not doing particularly well in high school in a few courses and not particularly caring, so I attended a small non-Ivy liberal arts school where I worked alongside many others in my same position, without pretense, but with much love for the pursuit of general knowledge. I never felt pressured to go in a certain direction; instead professors pushed me to ask big questions, to reason thoughtfully, and to approach each subject openly, using the knowledge I had garnered from other disciplines to contest theories and propose new ones. I remember while writing my honors thesis, which consequently did not exactly fit into my politics major, my advisers urged me to eschew the department guidelines and risk rejection, because, as they told me, it's not about the award, it's about the process of growth and learning and exploring that you will experience and take with you. I use that advice in everything I do.*

She is now enrolled, I should add, in a leading doctoral program, and in a different field than the one she majored in. Another young woman wrote this:

*Berry College in northeast Georgia gave me a full academic scholarship, and they had a beautiful campus, and a writing program, so I ended up there. It was a fortunate choice. Berry is small, and odd, and spottily brilliant, so it fit me perfectly. It has a few well-known professors—well perhaps only one—but the humanities program is chock-full of professors who are both intellectual and human, who are drawn to the chance to teach small classes of students who really care about ideas— and a few of them, the best, are quite charmingly half-insane by ordinary standards. The students, too, were something I'd not found before—people who actually cared about ideas, and books, and with whom I didn't feel as though I constantly had to withhold or hide my truest self, at least the intellectual side of it. At Berry I found something I haven't had in person before or since—a whole tight group of "kindred spirits," with whom I could regularly have intense conversations about literature or art or what it was like to be ourselves—and, particularly senior year as the "real world" encroached, our frequent communal existential crises were a relief to us all.*

**Teaching and the humanities: those** are the meat, the middle, of the liberal arts experience. But you should also look for colleges that pay attention to the ends. Avoid a school that's going to hand you a course catalogue when you walk in the door, pat you on the shoulder, and leave you to figure it out on your own. A couple of advising sessions aren't going to do it, either. What you want, ideally, is a dedicated freshman seminar—meaning more than just a writing class—that is designed to introduce you to the purpose of a college education.

There are many forms that such a course can take, but I learned of an exemplary version on a visit to Lawrence University, a liberal arts college in Wisconsin. Freshman Studies, a two-term sequence that's been taught since 1945, is presented as an "introduction to liberal learning." The course seeks to generate a sense of intellectual adventure as well as of intellectual community. The big questions, like what is the good life, are put directly on the table. While the syllabus is centered on the humanities, it draws from every branch of the curriculum. Einstein and Stephen Jay Gould keep company with Plato, Woolf, and Stravinsky. As one of the instructors said (and almost all of the instructors are professors, teaching in sections of fifteen), the course pushes kids beyond where they think they are disciplinarily. They discover that they have a love for history, or physics, or art.

It also helps them feel enfranchised. When I met with a group of seniors, they credited the class with enabling them to figure out what college is for. They had also clearly gotten the encouragement, and the tools, to be self-directed about their education. Their test scores may not have been as high as those of the kids I taught at Yale, but they seemed a lot more self-aware and certainly more at peace with their decisions. Out of their graduating class of 350, one of them boasted, only a handful were going to law school.

The end of college is equally important—and by the end, I don't mean graduation day. Look for a school that's going to take an active role in helping you to think about and make the transition to post-graduate life no matter what you major in. That means introducing you to as wide a range of options as possible. The process cannot wait until your senior year, shouldn't be an add-on, and needs to involve something more than the kind of half-assed approach, increasingly common, that tries to shoehorn professional skills (or worse, empty talk of "leadership") into the liberal arts classroom.

I'm not at all averse to active or service learning, courses and programs that put knowledge into practice and integrate study with extramural experiences. Reflection, again, should complement action, not gaze at its navel. Bennington, for instance, has redesigned its curriculum along exactly these lines. Students undertake a "plan process" that spans the four years and incorporates advising sessions, reflective essays, and the formulation of an individualized course of study. They do a seven-week "field work term" between semesters every year that helps to move them toward the postgraduate world in a mindful, systematic way. A Center for the Advancement of Public Action offers a range of interdisciplinary courses and gives students the opportunity to organize their education around specific issues such as poverty, public health, and the environment. The goal is to leverage learning as an agent of social change—the kind of objective that makes leadership and citizenship into something more than pretty words.

**What about skipping college altogether?** That's another fad these days—or at least, talking about it is. Bill Gates, Mark Zuckerberg: the same examples are invariably trotted out (though Gates and Zuckerberg attended Harvard for several semesters, and each made crucial contacts there). The venture capitalist Peter Thiel—bachelor's and law degrees from Stanford, the former as a philosophy major—has been offering fellowships for people under twenty to leave or forgo college to launch start-ups. Well, if you're a computer genius (or a tennis star—Steffi Graf has also been educed in this connection, which tells you how thoughtful the argument is), then that might be good advice. Otherwise it's pretty stupid. In purely financial terms—wage premiums, unemployment rates, lifetime earnings—college is not only still a good investment; according to a recent study, it is the best investment you can make. It is also a necessary credential for many kinds of work and any kind of professional training.

In terms of all the higher purposes that I've been talking about, it is equally indispensable. There may be brilliant autodidacts out there, people who need nothing but the world and a library (the writer Fran Lebowitz has said that she was glad to get kicked out of high school, because it gave her more time to read), but they're almost as rare as the Gateses and Zuckerbergs. Even Thoreau, the archetypal nonconformist, went to college, and may not have been Thoreau if he had not. It's true that college is imperfect even in the best of situations. Soul-making will never be strictly compatible with syllabi and semesters; imagination and courage do not fit neatly within rules and requirements. But if getting an inadequate education is bad, then getting none at all is even worse. You need to get a base, before you can take off on your own.

Far more significant than where you go to school, however, is why and how. What are you thinking about, as you make your college lists and do your tours? Never mind the fancy dorms and gyms; college shouldn't be a country club. What are the other students like? What are the teachers like? Look for schools where it's considered cool to think. Sit in on some classes, as prospective students almost never do. *U.S. News* has lists of "Best Undergraduate Teaching," too, and though they're based on the hearsay of reputational surveys (that is, the opinions of administrators at other schools), they may be worth at least a glance, if only since they have some names that don't show up as prominently on the main "Best Colleges" lists. Keep in mind that proxy statistics like student-faculty ratio or percentage of classes under twenty can be misleading. They don't tell you whether you actually get to see the faculty, or who is running those little classes. Go and find out for yourself.

Most of all, forget about the rankings, which drive so many bad decisions on the part of colleges and students both. Rankings lump together very different schools, make meaningless distinctions among essentially identical ones, and measure market position rather than educational quality. Go to a school you connect with, not, as students almost always do, the most prestigious one that lets you in.

Once you get there, keep your eye on the ball. You can't just passively absorb an education. Wherever you decide to go, you have to actively direct it. Look for teachers who devote themselves to their students, and don't be shy about approaching them outside of class. Look for courses, in whatever field, that want to humanize you, not specialize you. Follow your instincts wherever they lead. Choose a major that excites you: right now, about being a student. It's been said that college is the only situation where people want to get as little of what they pay for as possible. But this is your time; this is your shot. This is your chance to become, not the person that you want to be, not the person you've decided that you're going to be, but the person that you never could have dreamed of being. By far the most important factor, when you go to college, isn't the college. It's you.

# PART 4

*Society*

# Eleven

## Welcome to the Club

I've been speaking so far about what our system of elite education does to the people who go through it. Now we need to talk about what it's doing to the country as a whole. What it's doing, simply put, is reproducing the class system, just as it did in the bad old days of the Big Three a century ago. It is exacerbating inequality, retarding social mobility, perpetuating privilege, and creating an elite that is as isolated from the society that it's supposed to lead—and even more smug about its right to its position—as the WASP aristocracy itself.

The numbers are undeniable. In 1985, 46 percent of students at the 250 most selective colleges came from the top quarter of the income distribution. By 2000, it was 55 percent. By 2006 (albeit in a somewhat smaller sample), it was 67 percent. Only 15 percent came from bottom half that year; a slightly older study put the share of the bottom quarter at all of 3 percent. The more prestigious the school, the more unequal is its student body apt to be; Harvard, Yale, and Princeton, writes Jerome Karabel, "are still among the least economically diverse of the nation's major research universities." Public institutions, though, are not much better than the privates. As of 2004, 40 percent of students at the most selective state campuses came from families with incomes over $100,000, up from 32 percent just five years earlier. In the words of yet another study from the same year, "American higher education is more socioeconomically stratified today than at any time during the past three decades." The decade since, it's safe to say, has only made the situation worse.

The major reason for the trend is clear. Not increasing tuition, though that is a factor, but the ever-growing cost of manufacturing children who are fit to compete in the college admissions game. The more hurdles there are, the more expensive it is to catapult your kid across them. Tutors, test prep, and other ways of rigging the system are only the end of the process. Wealthy families, by pouring resources into their educational development, start buying their children's way into elite colleges almost from the moment they are born: music lessons, sports equipment, foreign travel ("enrichment" programs, to use the all-too-perfect word)—most important, of course, private school tuition or the costs of living in a place with top-tier public schools.

The SAT is supposed to measure aptitude; what it actually measures is parental income, with which it tracks quite closely, and even more, parental wealth, with which it tracks more closely still. The gap in academic skills between high- and low-income students has increased by about 40 percent over the last thirty years. The gap in college completion has grown even more—about 50 percent since the late 1980s. Less than half of high-scoring students from low-income families even *enroll* at four-year schools. (Stop and think about that for a minute.) As Paul Krugman put it, "smart poor kids are less likely than dumb rich kids to get a degree." The latter, said a former student—she was talking about the kids at her fancy private high school, every one of whom, even the biggest druggies and fuck-ups, are now doing fine—are "too rich to fail."

It is no coincidence that income inequality is higher than it's been since before the Great Depression, or that social mobility is now lower in the United States than in almost every other developed country. Colleges are not primarily to blame, but their policies do little to counteract these trends and a very great deal to make them worse. It's true that elite schools, especially the richest, have reached out more in recent years to low- and middle-income students. In 2007, Harvard made tuition free for families earning less than $60,000 and capped it at 10 percent of income for those earning up to $180,000 (which gives you an idea of what the middle class looks like from Cambridge). The percentage of kids on financial aid has gone up at a lot of the most selective schools, as has the portion of expenses covered by the average grant. Still, 40 percent of kids at Harvard, and even more at comparable schools, are continuing to pay full fare. An income of $180,000 puts you in the 94th percentile of households, which means that more than 40 percent of Harvard students come from the top 6 percent—maybe quite a bit more, since financial aid awards are not confined to those below the $180,000 threshold. Economic inequality leads to educational inequality, which leads to an applicant pool that is heavily skewed toward the rich.

But it isn't simply that there aren't more qualified lower-income kids from which to choose. Elite private colleges will never allow their students' economic profile to mirror that of society as a whole. They can't afford to, and it's not even clear that they'd want to. They need a critical mass of full payers, they need to tend to their donor base, and they need to serve their primary constituency, which is not the nation so much as the nation's—and increasingly, the world's—upper and upper middle classes: the classes from which their alumni come, to which their administrators belong, and for which their graduates are destined. One study found that a hundred high schools—about 0.3 percent of the nationwide total—account for 22 percent of students at Harvard, Yale, and Princeton. Of those hundred, all but six are private. The "feeder" system is alive and well.

Elite colleges are not just powerless to reverse the movement toward a more unequal society; their policies actively promote it. Claims to the contrary notwithstanding, selective schools give no admissions advantage to lower-income students, but they do give quite an advantage to other groups, most of whom are drawn disproportionately from the upper end of the income scale. In *The Price of Admission: How America's Ruling Class Buys Its Way into Elite Colleges* (a book I cannot read without wanting to vomit continuously), Daniel Golden describes these categories in detail: the children of donors, potential donors, and celebrities; faculty brats; and by far the largest, athletes and legacies, each of whom account for 10–25 percent of the typical student body at selective schools.

Legacies enjoy an average admissions advantage of 24 percent—which means that all other things being equal, their chances of getting in are that much greater—athletes, an advantage of 48 percent. The former category is a way of reproducing privilege more or less by definition, but one should not imagine that the latter is a way of counteracting it. Elite colleges typically field teams in more than two dozen sports; football and basketball are swamped, in the aggregate, by upper-class pursuits like squash, fencing, golf, crew, sailing, skiing, tennis, and polo. Title IX, Golden says, which mandates gender parity in college athletics, has basically become an affirmative action program for rich girls. "At least one-third of the students at elite universities, and at least half at liberal arts colleges," he writes, "are flagged for preferential treatment in the admissions process." And that, don't forget, is on top of the enormous academic advantages that affluent children already enjoy.

**It almost feels ridiculous to** have to insist that colleges like Harvard are bastions of privilege, places where the rich send their children to learn to walk, talk, and think like the rich, and to make sure that they stay rich—boarding schools, basically, for the 18–22-year-old set. Don't we all already know this? They aren't called elite colleges for nothing. But apparently we like pretending otherwise. We live in a meritocracy, after all. Doesn't everybody have an equal chance?

The sign of the system's alleged fairness, its break from the exclusionary past, is the set of policies that travel under the banner of "diversity." And that diversity does indeed represent nothing less than a social revolution. Princeton, which didn't even admit its first woman *graduate* student until 1961—a year in which a grand total of one (no doubt very lonely) African-American matriculated at its college—is now half female and only half white. But diversity of sex and race has become a cover, even an alibi, for increasing economic resegregation. Elite colleges are still living off the moral capital they earned in the 1960s, when they took the genuinely courageous step of dismantling the mechanisms of the WASP aristocracy. The truth is that the meritocracy was never more than partial. Remember that Kingman Brewster's reforms at Yale were immediately challenged by the school's alumni, who forced him to give way with respect, precisely, to athletes and legacies. (That the children of major donors would retain the largest advantage of all was never in question.) But now, even the essential meritocratic virtue of academic promise, as signified by the SAT and other criteria, has become a vehicle for the reproduction of privilege. Our new multiracial, gender-neutral meritocracy has figured out a way to make itself hereditary, and the education system is that way.

That is largely what "diversity" amounts to now. Visit any elite campus across our great nation, and you can thrill to the heart-warming spectacle of the children of white businesspeople and professionals studying and playing alongside the children of black, Asian, and Latino businesspeople and professionals. Kids at schools like Stanford think that their environment is diverse if one comes from Missouri, another one from Pakistan, or one plays the cello and the other one lacrosse—never mind that all of them have parents who are bankers or doctors. They aren't meeting "all kinds of people," as they like to say. They're meeting the same kind of people; they just happen to come from all kinds of places. They are "aware of themselves as an academic elite," as a former student wrote, "but not as a social (or economic) one."

That doesn't mean there aren't a few exceptions—partly since these schools are mindful of the need to justify their tax exemptions, partly since elites are always looking to refresh themselves with a little bit of new blood—but that is all they are. In fact, the group that is most disadvantaged by our current admissions policies (even more than Asians, who seem to be suffering a quota system that is similar to the one imposed on Jews a century ago) are working-class and rural whites, who are hardly present on selective campuses at all. The only way to think these places are diverse is if that's all you've ever seen.

Our educational system, it's been suggested, is what Americans developed in lieu of a European-style social welfare state to mitigate inequality. Instead of "handouts," opportunity. And once upon a time, it worked as advertised. Both the unprecedented expansion of public higher education and the equally unprecedented opening of access to the private sort were instrumental in creating a mass middle class, and a new upper and upper middle class, in the decades after World War II. But now instead of fighting inequality, the system has been captured by it.

The college admissions process, "complicated, publicly palatable, and elaborately costly," writes Mitchell L. Stevens in *Creating a Class*, is "the preponderant means of laundering privilege in contemporary American society." (The book, whose title alone should win a prize, is an in-depth account of the admissions process at a selective liberal arts college.) Despite the oceans of anxiety it generates, he adds, the ordeal endured by upper-middle-class seventeen-year-olds is "essentially ceremonial." What matters isn't how you do, but that you've been permitted to participate at all. The winners go to Brown; the losers go to Brandeis; the vast majority of kids, who never had a chance to play, go to Underfunded State University, or Budget Gulch Community College, or nowhere at all. As for programs like affirmative action or scholarship support, writes Walter Benn Michaels in *The Trouble with Diversity*, their actual purpose is to legitimate the system for those to whom they don't apply. "The function of the (very few) poor people at Harvard is to reassure the (very many) rich people at Harvard that you can't just buy your way into Harvard." American colleges and universities, he writes, are "propaganda machines" for the class structure.

If I were asked to give the freshman convocation speech at an elite college or university, those are the kinds of things I would say. You may be smart, I'd tell the students, you may be hardworking, but what you mainly are is very lucky. You outcompeted the kid who sat next to you at Stuyvesant or Harvard-Westlake, but 90 percent of your peers were excluded from the race before it even started.

What actually gets said on such occasions is exactly the reverse. Today's incoming freshmen, writes Andrew Delbanco, are invariably welcomed by the college president "with some version of the standard accolade: 'You are the most extraordinary class ever to walk through our gates.'" That is no exaggeration. A former student put it this way in an essay several years ago:

> *I would wager that most students in Yale's class of 2012 could give this year's admissions rate within a percentage point. . . . They certainly have no excuse for not knowing. I recall that everyone from President Levin to the freshman counselors mentioned my class's acceptance rate during orientation week— 9.9%, a record-breaker at the time. The implication of the statistic was clear: of all classes ever admitted to Yale, yours is the worthiest.*

Nor is that kind of language confined to undergraduate institutions, or to the United States. I've heard similar reports from people at the Kennedy School, Wharton, Princeton, the University of Toronto (one of the top-ranked schools in Canada), and the Pontifical Catholic University of Chile (one of the top-ranked schools in Latin America). An undergraduate wrote this in the *Harvard Crimson:*

> *Even before students uncap their pens for their first lecture; they are force-fed more praise than they know what to do with. . . . Depressingly, this type of proverbial back-patting makes it past ceremonious occasions like Commencement, filtering into the daily life of the classroom. . . . Just this week [less than a month into the semester], a professor told everyone in a fairly large class that we are already in the 99.9th percentile of people in the world who understand our specific area of content.*

It wasn't always thus. In the age of the WASP aristocracy, students heard a very different message. A former senior colleague wrote me as follows:

> *What was good about the bad old days was Yale's skeptical attitude towards its students. In the first weeks of September 1957, during some assembly or other, I remember the Dean of Yale College telling us that the pool of applicants from which we had been drawn was so large and so good that Yale could have recruited a class every bit as qualified as ours without offering admission to a single one of us. He went on to say that it was the duty of each of us over the next four years to prove that Yale had made the right choice by picking us instead of giving our place to someone else. I returned to Yale as a faculty member in 1969, and by then the change had already taken place. By then deans were telling each entering class that they were the most wonderful set of human beings who had ever entered Yale, and how wonderful it was for Yale that they had decided to attend.*

What had happened, of course, was the shift to meritocracy. Schools have lots of reasons for stroking their students' egos. It makes for happy customers. It primes the donation pump. Along with all the ceremonies of belonging—the convocations and initiations and commencements, the branded swag of sweatshirts and window stickers, the "great [your school's name here] traditions," the tribal bonding of athletic rivalry, the whole cultus of alma materism—it helps to build the loyalty the institutions will be milking for the balance of their students' lives. But mainly they do it because they believe it. The flattery in question is essentially reflexive: you're great because we're great. (One of my students has written of "Yale's boundless appetite for self-celebration.") Administrators and professors, after all, are products of the meritocracy themselves, and their presence at an elite institution is a never-ending source of self-delight. Their sense of identity—of the world, of society, of justice—is built upon the same equation as their students': you're here because you earned it, and you earned it because you're the best.

Such thinking, of course, is the essence of the elite mentality, the "hot shit" part of the dynamic. It's the pact that you sign up for when you learn to see yourself in terms of scores and grades. The problem isn't that those measures are imperfect (though they are). The problem is that students are incessantly encouraged to believe that academic excellence is excellence, full stop, that better at school means simply better—better morally, better metaphysically, higher on some absolute scale of human value.

There is nothing wrong with taking pride in your intellect or achievement. There *is* something wrong with the smugness and self-congratulations that elite schools connive at from the moment that the fat envelopes arrive in the mail. The message is implicit in every tone of voice and tilt of the head, every article in the student paper, every one of those old-school traditions. The message is, you have arrived. Welcome to the club. And the corollary is equally clear: you deserve everything your presence here is going to enable you to get. When people say that students at elite schools have a sense of entitlement, that is what they are referring to: the belief that you deserve more than other people because your SAT scores are higher. Of course, your SAT scores are higher because you have already gotten more than other people.

When I wrote my original article about the disadvantages of an elite education, I started with a story about my plumber. I was thirty-five; it was the first time I had called a tradesman as a homeowner. What I discovered that day, as he stood there in the kitchen preparing to get down to work, was that I had no idea how to speak to him. So alien was his experience to me, so unguessable his values, so mysterious his very language, that I couldn't succeed in engaging him in a couple of minutes of small talk. Fourteen years of higher education, and there I was, stiff and stupid, struck dumb by my own dumbness. I could carry on conversations with people from other countries, in other languages, but I didn't know what to say to the man who was standing in my own house.

A lot of readers objected to the story as a portrait of the elite predicament—to the idea, as I said, that one disadvantage of an elite education is that it makes you incapable of talking to people who aren't exactly like you, for the simple reason that you never meet any. *They* don't have trouble talking to their plumbers, they insisted. Well, maybe not; maybe I was unusually handicapped in that respect. I not only grew up in an upper-middle-class suburban neighborhood; I was raised in an Orthodox Jewish community and attended parochial schools for most of my childhood. But I also know that people do not often see themselves too clearly when it comes to things like this—to their class position and how it's cut them off from those around them. You may not be quite as down with the regular folks as you like to believe.

I know as well that the way I was raised, religion aside, is, if anything, increasingly common. Bill Bishop has written about "the big sort": our ongoing process of self-segregation by mind-set and lifestyle—which really means, by economic status. The stalling of social mobility and migration of the affluent to upscale enclaves, and of their children to private schools or might-as-well-be-private public ones, ensure that the isolation of the upper classes starts not in college, but at birth. The kind of narrow, sheltered upbringing I experienced is now, for the kids who make it to the most selective institutions, pretty much the norm. They aren't meeting any "plumbers," either.

But the problem isn't only isolation. The logic of "better" is perfectly clear. An elite education doesn't simply fail to teach you how to talk to people who are genuinely different than you; it tells you that you shouldn't even bother. Forget about class. The message is that anyone who didn't go to a prestigious school is not worth wasting time with, regardless of their class. You are "the best and the brightest," as these places love to say, and everybody else is, well, something else: less good, less bright, and in any case, beneath you. "One friend of mine recalled taking the T into Boston," a Harvard student wrote me, "and, while looking at the other passengers, feeling that these people, who could never hope to be her intellectual equals, simply didn't exist in the way that a member of the Harvard community did."

None of this is inconsistent either with the notion of service or with the crippling insecurity that also comes with the elite mentality. In fact, it is perfectly consistent with both. The whole idea of "service," as embodied in organizations like Teach For America and among the elite in general, is inherently condescending. You do for others—those poor, unfortunate others—what you don't think they can do for themselves. You swoop down and rescue them with your awesome wisdom and virtue. You *do* acknowledge their existence, but in a fashion that maintains your sense of superiority—indeed, that reinforces it.

As for insecurity, it is just the other half, the piece-of-shit component, of the elite dynamic. Contempt, says Alice Miller in *The Drama of the Gifted Child* (in a section called "The Loneliness of the Contemptuous"), is a defense against feelings of inadequacy:

> As long as we despise the other person and overvalue our own achievements ("he can't do what I can do"), we do not have to mourn the fact that love is not forthcoming without achieve-

*ment. Nevertheless, if we avoid this mourning it means that we remain at bottom the one who is despised, for we have to despise everything in ourselves that is not wonderful, good, and clever.*

Remember Amy Chua, how necessary "losers" were to her psychic equilibrium. "Losers" embody the rejected parts of the self, the fate that you secretly dread. Their presence—if only their imaginative presence—is a constant salve, a mental resource you can always draw upon to restore those fragile, precious feelings of hot-shitness. That is why the entitlement of meritocrats is so distant from the genuine self-confidence of the old aristocracy. Entitlement is always anxious, always selfish, always shadowed by the fear of failure.

Some years ago, the social scientist Jean Anyon published an article titled "Social Class and the Hidden Curriculum of Work." Surveying five New Jersey elementary schools, she concluded that the ways in which students are taught, even more than what they are taught, prepare them to occupy their respective class positions. Working-class kids are heavily disciplined and instructed by rote; the sons and daughters of professionals get creativity and self-expression; the children of the business class are taught authority, mastery, and self-control.

College isn't any different. An elite education not only ushers you into the upper reaches of society; it trains you for the life that you'll be leading once you get there. "When Yale offers free fellowships to study in China or subsidizes a trip to New York to catch a Broadway show," a former student wrote, "it bills these luxuries as instruction in how to be broad-minded and cultured. The truth is that they are, more than anything else, instruction in how to be wealthy."

I didn't grasp this principle until I began to compare my experience, and even more, my students' experience, with that of a friend who went to Cleveland State. My friend had once received a D for the semester—she'd been running an A in the class—because she was coming off a waitressing shift and had to hand her final paper in an hour late. That may be an extreme example, but it's one that is unthinkable at schools like Yale. There are due dates and attendance requirements at elite colleges, but no one takes them very seriously. Extensions are available for the asking; threats to deduct credit for missed classes are rarely, if ever, carried out. Kids at prestigious schools, in other words, receive an endless string of second chances.

Just as unthinkably, my friend had no one to appeal to. Students at places like Cleveland State are not supported by a platoon of advisors and tutors and deans to write out excuses for late work, give them extra help when they need it, or pick them up when they fall down. They get their education wholesale, from an indifferent bureaucracy, not handed them in gift-wrapped packages by smiling clerks. They have little opportunity for the kinds of contacts that I saw my students get routinely—classes with visiting power brokers, dinners with foreign dignitaries. There are also few, if any, of the sorts of special funds that prestigious schools dispense in such profusion: travel stipends, research fellowships, performance grants. Each year, my old department gives out literally dozens of cash prizes for everything from senior theses down to freshman essays. In 2009, those prizes came to well over one hundred thousand dollars—in one department alone.

Students at schools like Cleveland State also don't get A-minuses just for doing the work. The most egregious thing about grade inflation is how uneven it has been. As of the 1950s, the average GPA was comparable at public and private institutions, about a 2.5. Then the numbers began to diverge. By 2007, the average grade had risen to a 3.01 at public schools, but at private schools it had risen to a 3.30, and at highly selective private schools, a 3.43. Only in the Ivy

League and places like it does the A-minus constitute a sort of default setting, the point from which one either rises or sinks. It's not a grade so much as a metaphor, the emblem of entitled mediocrity. It means, don't worry, we'll take care of you.

Students at places like Cleveland State—and I've confirmed these observations with people who have worked at comparable schools—are being trained to occupy positions somewhere in the middle of the class system, in the depths of one bureaucracy or other. They're being conditioned for lives with few second chances, no extensions, little support, narrow opportunity—lives of subordination, supervision, and control, lives of deadlines, not guidelines. For students at prestigious schools, it is exactly the reverse: connections, freebies, privileges, access. And one more thing: impunity. Not only is the meritocracy imperfect to begin with; it only functions up to a point. Getting through the door is very difficult, but once you're in, there's almost nothing you can do to get yourself kicked out. Not the worst academic failure, not the most egregious act of plagiarism, not even threatening a fellow student with bodily harm—I have heard of all three—is sufficient to get you expelled. Once you've been admitted to the club, the feeling seems to be, you've got a God-given right to stay in the club.

This isn't just the self-protection of the old boys' network, updated to include the other sex. It is actually much worse. Here is my former colleague again, the one who got to Yale in 1957:

*The attitude of the administration towards us was backed by an uncorrupted grading system. If you screwed up in a course, you got the equivalent of an F, and if you got very many of them, you were out. Roughly 10–15% of every class in that era left Yale without a degree. It was not quite "look at the man to the left of you and look at the man to your right, in four years only two of you will still be here," but it had that flavor. In short, we lived in a world where privilege was accompanied by responsibility. I would submit that Yale was right to challenge us this way, and that no 18-year-old should ever be encouraged to think that he or she has already got it made.*

But that was then. That Harvard student who was studying self-efficacy also spoke to me about the "yes culture" she experienced at college. The sense that Harvard instilled that you were capable of doing anything, she said, was rooted in the fact that the school said "yes" to whatever you wanted. If you hoped to study, say, in China for a year, the money was there; all you had to do was raise your hand. I didn't mention that there might be some connection there to grade inflation, but I did let her know that what she had said was more or less the definition of entitlement. We're not entitled, she said; we work hard. Yes, I said, but working hard is not enough. Reward should go to achievement, not simply effort or desire. She countered that she had a friend who applied for the Rhodes despite the fact that you're supposed to need at least a 3.9 and he had only had a 3.6, and she thought that that was great. I said, a kid who has a 3.6 doesn't deserve to get a Rhodes. She thought *that* was elitist: someone with a 3.6 *should* have a shot at the Rhodes, if they wanted it badly enough. In other words, no limits ever.

We're not entitled, we work hard—that's the rationale one often hears. And you may indeed have worked much harder than the kids around you, but what about the ones you couldn't see? Do you really think that none of *them* worked hard? What about the kid at the public school a couple of towns over, who put in just as many hours every week, only twenty-five of them were at a Denny's? The way things go at this point, being treated fairly is itself a form of privilege. Most Americans work hard *without* receiving the rewards they've earned. That, in fact, is pretty much what social inequality involves today.

A former community college student and Marine combat veteran, later a student at Stanford, had this to say about the bubble that surrounds the bulk of kids who end up at prestigious schools:

*It's useful to think of Stanford students (and their peers around the country and world) as flowers in a garden. Many tend them— parents, counselors, test prep specialists, teachers, professors, friends—and they generally bloom in response to such careful cultivation. These flowers, while beautiful, are young and fragile and must be sheltered from the elements. Thank goodness for the constant gardening.*

*I am a weed in their garden, masquerading as a flower. I can't be told stories about the world outside the garden by the gardeners because I've been further and seen more than any of them. I am calloused and don't respond to the regimen of organic diet, self-congratulatory volunteer work, and politically correct pillow talk that grows so many other young leaders of the free world. I grew my roots slowly, painfully, in the dry rocky soil of the real world.*

*I don't mean to romanticize such a life, only say that the hardier plants grow to be much stronger than is possible in the garden. But why leave the vibrant colors, constant distractions, and beautifully simple garden for a morally ambiguous (even dangerous) outside world? Here the patterns of life are essentially known: you do A, you get B. But what if the world didn't help ensure B followed from A? What would our poor flower do then?*

**Is there anything that I** can do, a lot of young people have written to ask me, to avoid becoming an out-of-touch, entitled little shit? I don't have a satisfying answer, short of telling you to transfer to a public university. You cannot cogitate your way to sympathy with people of different backgrounds, still less to knowledge of them. You need to interact with them directly, and it has to be on an equal footing: not in the context of "service," and not in the spirit of "making an effort," either—swooping down on a member of the college support staff, say, and offering to buy them a cup of coffee, as somebody suggested in rebuttal to my article, so you can "get to know them." The only way to treat somebody as an equal is to realize that that's exactly what they are.

Instead of service, how about service *work*? That'll really give you insight into other people. How about waiting tables yourself, so you can see how hard it is, not only physically but mentally? You really aren't as smart as everyone's been telling you; you're only smarter in a certain way, and only than your peers in the propertied class. There are smart people who do not go to a prestigious college, or to any college, and often precisely for reasons of class. There are smart people who are not "smart." You've heard that there are different forms of intelligence? Now go and find it out through actual experience. A former student who got a job at a community college after graduation had this to report about the people who went there: "The students are incredibly diverse in all possible ways, some of them very obviously in need of help and others who make me feel young, coarse, and just plain stupid." The "best" are the brightest only in a narrow sense.

I know it's hard to hear these things as a privileged young person. It was very hard for me to hear them, when the knowledge started to be thrust upon me. It's not your fault you grew up affluent and sheltered. But now you need to take responsibility for it. You can start by recognizing that you aren't, in fact, more valuable than other people, no matter what you've always heard. Your pain does not hurt more. Your soul does not weigh more. If I were religious, I would say that

God does not love you more. And the social implications should be clear. As John Ruskin told an earlier elite, grabbing everything you can isn't any more virtuous when you do it with the power of your brains than it is when you do it with the power of your fists. "Work must always be," he said, "and captains of work must always be," but "there is a wide difference between being captains or governors of work, and taking the profits of it."

Yet that is exactly what's happening now, to an extent we haven't seen in more than eighty years: our "leaders," the elite, who are supposed to work for the greater good, enrich themselves at everyone else's expense and justify their actions with the notion that they're "better." Not being an entitled little shit is an admirable goal, but the real problem is the situation that makes it so hard to be anything else. The real problem, once again, is the system itself. How, at last, to change it is the subject of my final chapter.

# Twelve

## The Self-Overcoming
## of the Hereditary Meritocracy

"The best and the brightest": what a perfect irony that hoary old cliché entails. Nobody apparently remembers that the phrase originated as the rancidly sarcastic title of a book about the architects of the Vietnam War—the so-called "whiz kids" whose arrogance and overconfidence enmeshed us in a quagmire. The best and the brightest, indeed: Has there ever been a leadership class more pleased with itself than our own? Has there ever been another one whose failure is more obvious? The contemporary meritocracy, which in all its glory is presiding over an era of unprecedented national decline, is an exact reflection of the educational system that is charged with reproducing it. The time has come, not simply to reform that system top to bottom, but to begin to plot our exit to another form of leadership, another kind of society, altogether.

The meritocracy purports, like every ruling class, to act for the good of all. Its ethos is in fact, by definition, one of self-advancement: not duty or responsibility, not character or even leadership, but individual aggrandizement, a single-minded focus on the self and its success. And yet the meritocracy believes, again by definition, in its own superior virtue. That's what "merit" means, after all. The word has moral connotations that are absent from the ones we might imagine in its place—"intelligence" or "aptitude," even "excellence" or "achievement." The spiritual overtones it carried in the Middle Ages echo in our use of it today. "Meritocracy": we are ruled by a kind of elect. Every leadership class evolves an ideology that justifies its own position. The WASPs had social Darwinism, the idea that the Nordic races governed the world by virtue of having prevailed in the struggle for survival. Now we have people like Charles Murray, in *The Bell Curve*, telling us about the "cognitive elite" and the heritability of intelligence. And if some reject what seems like social Darwinism in a new guise, they silently substitute effort for aptitude, diligence for genetic endowment. Like my Harvard student, they tell themselves that they deserve their status because they (unlike everybody else, apparently) *work hard*. Either way, the poor are poor because they are inferior. The affluent and powerful have "merit."

Our most recent presidential race afforded an extended lesson in the elite mentality in the person of the Republican nominee. I don't mean only his infamous remark about the 47 percent. Equally revealing was the candidate's suggestion about the unemployment crisis: that recent graduates should borrow money from their parents to start a business. "In the old days," the novelist Julian Barnes has a character reflect, "there had been tribes wandering around who believed they were the only tribe on earth, and whose belief was not shaken by the appearance of other tribes. People who were called successes reminded Gregory of these tribes." For those like Mitt Romney, on some emotional level, those who are not like Mitt

Romney, as that other Harvard student felt about the people on the T, simply don't exist.

They know they're out there, but they can't imagine what their lives are like, and despite the fact that they're allowed to make decisions that affect them deeply, they aren't much interested in trying. They suffer, yes, from Plumber's Syndrome, as we might refer to it, or in a friend's unfortunate but pungent phrase, Ivy Retardation. And if Romney seems like an extreme example of our out-of-touch elite, consider the two Democratic nominees who preceded our current president, Al Gore and John Kerry: one each from Harvard and Yale, both earnest, decent, intelligent men, both utterly unable to communicate with the larger electorate. In fact, consider our current president— a graduate of Honolulu's prestigious Punahou School as well as of Columbia and Harvard Law—who despite his race, his oratorical skills, and his years as a community organizer, is equally incapable of making an emotional connection with the people he calls "folks."

As for his predecessor, that apotheosis of entitled mediocrity, he is another perfect product of the system we've evolved to train our leaders. Entitled mediocrity was indeed the operating principle of his entire administration, but as the last dozen years or more have demonstrated on a daily basis, it is now the operating principle of our leadership class as a whole. Not only are our institutions comprehensively failing (George Packer has written about the Iraq War as a stress test that revealed the weakness of "the executive and legislative branches, the military, the intelligence world, the for-profits, the nonprofits, the media"; in *Twilight of the Elites*, Christopher Hayes refers to the last ten years more broadly as the "fail decade"), but no one, as we know, is being held responsible. For the elite, there is always another extension: a bailout, a pardon, a stint in rehab. The fat salaries awarded to underperforming CEOs are an adult version of the A-minus. Anyone who remembers the injured sanctimony with which the head of Enron, Kenneth Lay, received the notion that he should be punished for his crimes will understand the sense of impunity under which our leaders now conduct themselves. But you don't need to remember Kenneth Lay, because the whole tragic farce has been playing out again, in massive, Technicolor detail, on Wall Street.

George W. Bush, however, did get one thing right: his diagnosis of his own predecessor and, if only inadvertently, of the type to which he belongs. "Our current president," said Bush of Bill Clinton in his first convention speech, "embodied the potential of a generation. So many talents. So much charm. Such great skill. But, in the end, to what end? So much promise, to no great purpose." "Purpose" is a word we've seen before. If Bush was feckless privilege personified, Clinton epitomized the unfocused ambition that the system cultivates so well. Every presidential candidate—everyone who rises high in any field— will be enormously ambitious of necessity. In Clinton's case, as in so many others', it was painfully clear that that is all he was. He knew what he wanted, but he had no idea why.

I also think of the kind of figures with which the last several administrations, as well as our institutions in general, have been so abundantly stocked: people like Condoleezza Rice, that perfect bureaucratic cipher, or Elena Kagan, who made it all the way to the Supreme Court without depositing a paper trail—resume jockeys devoid of discernible passion carefully maneuvering their way to the top. Is it any wonder that our country has itself appeared to lose all sense of purpose, when our leaders have none of their own? Once, we dreamed of eradicating poverty, winning the Cold War, reaching the moon, ensuring racial justice, creating a more equitable society. Now—what? What large national project are we pursuing, or even talking of pursuing? So much freedom. So much wealth and power. Such technological sophistication. But in the end, to what end?

Brilliant, gifted, energetic, yes, but also anxious, greedy, bland,

and risk-averse, with no courage and no vision—that is our elite today. The meritocracy is also a technocracy. It can solve the problems that you put in front of it, but it cannot tell you whether they're the right ones to be working on. It is trained to operate within the system, never to imagine that we might create a better one. It is oblivious to beliefs, values, and principles—the things the humanities teach you to think about—because it takes them so much for granted that it ceases to remember they exist. It is bereft of intellectual resources more nutritious than today's op-ed or yesterday's position paper. It is the rule of experts, or in the words of Saul Bellow, "high-IQ morons"—people lacking in "a wider thoughtfulness." We do need experts, to be sure, but we also need them not to be in charge.

And here I fear I have to quote another Bush, the elder one. His 1988 opponent, Michael Dukakis (Swarthmore, Harvard Law), the first of the meritocratic major-party presidential nominees, had famously announced, in his own convention address, that "this election isn't about ideology; it's about competence"—the technocrat's creed in a nutshell. To which the first George Bush replied: "Competence makes the trains run on time but doesn't know where they're going." What the election *should* be about, he added—what everyone should be about—is, precisely, beliefs, values, and principles.

The great exemplar of the technocrat, however, is not the hapless Dukakis, a high-IQ moron if there ever was one, but our current president himself. His book was called *The Audacity of Hope,* but only his ambition is audacious. A centrist, a pragmatist, a seeker of consensus: he plays it safe, like every other product of the system. He seeks to wear the mantle of the visionary, but his vision is technocracy itself—those "common sense" solutions that he always likes to talk about. If politics is the art of the possible, Obama's failure as a leader is precisely his conception of what is possible, his meek acceptance of the limits of the status quo.

Like a student who's afraid to take a course he might do poorly in, he dodges the difficult fights. If that analogy seems strained, consider that he actually maintains a list of his achievements (yes, really), and that he gave himself a 70 for his first two years in office (that is, he thinks that he accomplished 70 percent of what he had hoped to achieve). He's grading himself, in other words, and on a rather generous curve—almost too perfect a metaphor for the meritocratic mind-set. The electorate, that year of 2010, was less impressed, though the outcome came to him, apparently, as quite a shock. Incapable of comprehending the developing disaster, which has crippled the rest of his presidency, he seemed to think he'd ace the midterms (the confluence of terminology is sweet) if he only got the answers right.

He also couldn't understand why people might object to some of his appointments—figures like Timothy Geithner or Larry Summers, both of whom were central to creating the conditions that led to the financial crisis. They're "the best," after all; whom else would you choose to run the economy? Obama's arrogance and that of his advisors, as ill-concealed as it has proved to be unearned, is that of the double-800 crowd. It's as if he can't believe that anybody might reject those commonsense solutions once he has explained them carefully enough—as if he has no conception of competing values, interests, or perspectives, no idea that society is more than just equations. With his racial identity and relatively humble background, his election has been called the triumph of the meritocracy. The sad thing is that that's exactly what it was.

**I've been considering our recent** presidential candidates as examples of the failures of the meritocracy, but the most remarkable fact is that so many have been products of the system in the first place.

There have been ten major-party presidential nominees since 1988. All but two, Bob Dole and John McCain, attended elite private colleges, and seven of the remaining eight went on to elite professional schools. All eight—both Bushes, Dukakis, Clinton, Gore, Kerry, Obama, and Romney—attended Harvard or Yale at some point in their education.

Compare this to the fourteen nominees from 1948 to 1984, the heyday of the public university. Only three went to elite private colleges, and only two were associated with Harvard or Yale at any point (a third went to Princeton). Eight, more than half, attended state schools, as compared to only one from 1988 to 2012. Richard Nixon went to Whittier College. Ronald Reagan went to Eureka College. Lyndon Johnson went to Southwest Texas State Teachers College. Barry Goldwater didn't finish college. Harry Truman didn't go to college.

It is also striking what a large proportion of our recent nominees are legacies. From 1948 to 1984, only two were. Since then, fully six of ten have been: both Bushes, Gore, Kerry, McCain, and Romney— sons of senators, a president, a governor, an admiral, and in Kerry's case, a foreign service officer who went to Andover, Yale, and Harvard (as well as a mother whose last name was Forbes). Over the last four cycles, the proportion has been even higher—five of six. (Hillary Clinton versus Jeb Bush or Rand Paul in 2016 would make it seven of eight.) This is not an anomaly, as the previous chapter made clear; this is how the system works.

What we see in the presidency we see throughout today's elite. Eight of nine Supreme Court justices received their law degrees from Harvard or Yale, an unprecedented number, and six of nine received their undergraduate degrees from Harvard, Stanford, or Princeton. As of 2011, just a single member of the cabinet had gone to college at a public institution. According to the 2002 edition of *Who's Running America*, 54 percent of leaders in the corporate world and 42 percent of those in government have degrees from one or more of only twelve universities. Elite graduate programs are heavily biased toward a relatively small number of colleges, and private firms increasingly recruit from only a handful or two. A recent study found that the most prestigious law firms, investment banks, and consultancies will scarcely look at you unless you went to Harvard, Yale, Princeton, possibly Stanford, or if you have an MBA, the Wharton School. Even places like MIT, Columbia, and Dartmouth are considered second-rate.

Given the profusion of excellent colleges, as well as the increasing pool of gifted students who are shut out of the HYPSters or the Golden Dozen, what accounts for this demented exclusivity? The same mentality that drives the system as a whole. People who attended top-ranked institutions simply don't believe that those who didn't might be valuable enough to hire or admit. The study I just mentioned speaks of "a culture that's insanely obsessed with pedigree." Hiring someone from Harvard or Princeton is also safe. If they prove to be a dud, you can't be blamed for having selected them. No one has the fortitude to play a hunch or take a chance.

In view of the fact that the system churns out an endless procession of more or less uniform human specimens, you'd think that places might prefer to have some different minds around—or more to the point, some different personalities. If the elite got any more inbred, they'd start to grow tails. No wonder the people who run our institutions, despite their fabulous credentials, have all been making the same mistakes, and making them over and over. The result, in any case, is that the country as a whole is effectively "tracked" from grade school on—or really, from the womb.

But the meritocracy is not just self-enclosed and self-perpetuating; it is also self-dealing. Everywhere we look, we witness people in authority abusing their positions to the detriment of those they're pledged to serve. Doctors take money from drug companies to puff and push their products even when safer and cheaper alternatives are available. College presidents permit themselves enormous salaries at a time of ballooning tuitions and straitened budgets. Politicians give up office to line their pockets as lobbyists; regulators leave to take positions with the firms they used to oversee. Executives loot their companies; investment banks conspire against their clients; accounting firms and credit rating agencies cook the books. Our leadership class, in short, has turned its back upon the rest of us. It is no coincidence that the age of the meritocracy, for all the liberal pretensions of so many of its members, has also been the age of Reaganism. Their logic is the same: every man for himself.

No one appears to grasp that leadership involves responsibility as well as opportunity. No one seems to realize that it isn't all about their fabulous lifestyles. Lewis Lapham speaks of "a managerial elite loyal to nothing other than its own ambition." Its poster child is Tony Hayward, erstwhile CEO of BP, best remembered for whining, in the middle of one of the greatest environmental disasters in history, that he wanted his life back. His company was despoiling an entire region, and the only person he was capable of feeling sorry for was Tony Hayward.

We have been here before. "History," said E. Digby Baltzell in *The Protestant Establishment*, "is a graveyard of classes which have preferred caste privilege to leadership." His classic study of the Anglo-Saxon aristocracy, which put the term "WASP" into general circulation, was published in 1964, the very year that Yale was revolutionizing its admissions practices, Year One of the meritocracy. The owl of Minerva, as the saying goes, was spreading its wings at dusk: a historical phenomenon was receiving its definitive articulation at the very moment of its passage from the scene.

But the end had been coming for decades. The WASP ascendancy had reached its peak in the 1920s, which Baltzell calls "the Anglo-Saxon decade." The period was also, as we know, an age of frenzied excess, the last time inequality attained the proportions it has once again assumed today. The end of World War I had functioned in something of the way that the collapse of the Soviet empire later would. Global leadership had passed to the United States—which means, to the WASPs. We also know what happened next. "The destinies of the world were handed them on a plate in 1920," Baltzell quotes a member of that class as having said. "Their piglike rush for immense profits knocked over the whole feast in nine years."

When James B. Conant, the president of Harvard, began the move to meritocracy in the early 1930s, the depths of the Depression, the ruling class was dealing with the need, not only to enfranchise rising groups and mobilize the nation's talent, but also to face its own catastrophic failure. The Crash of 1929 had represented a crisis of legitimacy, the moment that the aristocracy was seen to have outlived its usefulness. The end was long in coming, but the WASPs, to their everlasting credit, did do one thing right before they left the stage—or at least, enough of them did. However slowly and reluctantly, out of whatever mixture of motives, they prepared the ground for their own supersession. They overcame themselves. They put the interests of the nation as a whole above their own, for they had come to recognize the two were not the same. They saw, at least eventually, that a new and very different ruling class would have to take their place.

The parallels today are striking. The aristocracy and meritocracy each persisted for about the same amount of time before the smash: the former from the 1880s to 1929, the latter from the 1960s to 2008. But other things are different. No one, it seems—no one in authority, at least—has learned the lesson of the recent crisis. The lesson is not about financial regulation or legal accountability. The lesson is, it's time to move along. It's time for the hereditary meritocracy—not just the 1 percent, the plutocracy, but the 10–15 percent, the elite as a whole, professionals as well as bankers, liberals as well as conservatives, the upper middle and the upper classes both—to start to undertake its own self-overcoming. The system isn't working anymore, no matter how just or good or inevitable it seems to those it flatters and benefits. It has lost its authority. It has lost its legitimacy. It is time to imagine what a different society would look like, and to gather the courage to get there.

The new dispensation must ensure—this is the essential thing—that privilege cannot be handed down. The education system has to act to mitigate the class system, as it did in the middle decades of the twentieth century, not reproduce it. We can certainly begin with the admissions process, just as they did in the 1930s. Affirmative action should be based on class instead of race, a change that many have been calling for for years. Preferences for legacies and athletes ought to be discarded. SAT scores should be weighted to account for socio-economic factors—a plan that was developed (and needless to say, rejected) in 1990. Colleges should put an end to resume-stuffing by imposing a limit on the number of extracurriculars that kids can list on their applications. They ought to place more value on the kind of service jobs that lower-income students often take in high school (and that high achievers almost never do). They should refuse to be impressed by any experience or opportunity that was enabled by parental wealth. Of course, they have to stop cooperating with *U.S. News*.

More broadly, they need to rethink their conception of merit. If schools are going to train a better class of leaders than the ones we have today, they're going to have to ask themselves what kinds of qualities they need to promote and how to select for them. Once admissions criteria change, the whole educational system will change. We want kids with resilience, self-reliance, independence of spirit, genuine curiosity and creativity, and a willingness to take risks and make mistakes. A student who worked in the admissions office at Pomona told me that her favorite applicants to interview were the interesting ones who had failed a little in high school—but no, she said, they never got in. Some have suggested that applicants be asked to submit a "failure resume" along with their list of accomplishments. David Brooks has remarked, apropos of the groupthink that grips the establishment, that our institutions don't reward "cantankerous intellectual bomb-throwers." Well, that's exactly who we need to start rewarding.

Colleges should remember that selecting students by GPA more often benefits the faithful drudge than the original mind. The same goes for quantity as opposed to quality—of APs, extracurriculars, and so forth. Excellence requires single-mindedness as well as the freedom to follow one's intuition, not a willingness to fill in every box. Helen Vendler, the Harvard professor and dean of American poetry critics, has tried to remind her institution that great artists are not likely to be "leaders" or the kinds of people who are good at everything (or want to be), and I would say the same about great scientists, great thinkers, and great just about everything else. When Yale set out to reform its admissions in the 1960s, it sought to get away from the bland, predictable prep school types and find instead some "brilliant and restless minds." But by now we have evolved a different kind of blandness. Who would describe the typical Ivy League student today as intellectually restless? Who would even say that more than a few are brilliant—an altogether different thing than being very bright. Forget about the A-minuses; even the A's are boring now. We desperately need some A-pluses, and if that means taking some admissions chances, and making some mistakes, so be it.

The meritocracy developed in a very different world, and its educational system was designed for a very different economy. The postwar age was one of large bureaucratic institutions staffed by cadres of scientific and social-scientific experts. It was the age of the Ford Motor Company and the Ford Foundation, of NASA and the Pentagon and Bell Labs, and it looked like it would last forever. The notion of sorting everybody on the basis of a single test and training them to occupy a slot in the social machine made a terrifying kind of sense. The postwar years were also the age of the Cold War, a static global system that placed a premium on managing the status quo, and one that likewise looked to be eternal. But now we face a world of economic fluidity, political instability, and unpredictable dangers and opportunities. We need a different kind of brain.

**The changes must go deeper,** though, than just reforming the admissions process at selective schools. That might address the problem of mediocrity, but it won't address the greater one of inequality. Private colleges and universities will only ever go so far in opening their gates to the poor and middle class, for the simple reason that they cannot afford to do otherwise. We need instead to overhaul the entire way we organize our higher education system. The problem isn't this or that admissions practice; the problem is the Ivy League itself—the position it and other schools have been allowed to occupy. The problem is that we have contracted the training of our leadership class to a set of private institutions. However much they claim to act, or think they're acting, for the common good, they will always place their interests first. They will always be the creatures of the rich. The arrangement is great for the schools, whose wealth and influence continue to increase, but is Harvard's desire for alumni donations a sufficient reason to perpetuate the class system? I used to think that we needed to create a world where every child had an equal chance to get to the Ivy League. I've come to see that what we really need is to create one where you don't have to go to the Ivy League, or any private college, to get a first-rate education.

This is not a new idea. It is the exact commitment that drove the growth of public higher education in the postwar years. When Nelson Rockefeller, governor of New York and one of the last of the WASP aristocrats, undertook a vast expansion of his state's university system, he did so, he said, because he thought that every citizen deserved an education that was just as good as the one that he'd received at Dartmouth. California created one of the greatest systems in the world, a virtual West Coast Ivy League, on the basis of the same idea. Public education, financed with public money, for the benefit of all. Everybody gets an equal chance to go as far as their hard work and talent will take them (you know, the American dream). Everyone who wants it gets to have the kind of mind-expanding, soul-enriching experience that a liberal arts education provides. We recognize that free, quality K–12 education is a human right. We also need to recognize—as we once did and as many countries still do—that the same is true of higher education.

So what became of that commitment? Basically, we decided that we didn't want to have to pay for it anymore. Instead of taxes, student loans. By the time the recession began, higher education spending as a share of state budgets had dropped by about a third since 1980. Since 2008, it has fallen another 18 percent in absolute terms, nearly 30 percent or more in several major states. It is no coincidence that public university tuitions have increased at over 5 percent a year during the past decade, more than twice as fast as at the privates (where real student costs have actually been flat). Since 1989, state expenditure on higher education per dollar of personal income—the part, in other words, that comes from us—has dropped by almost half. During roughly the same period, the share of revenue at public universities that's covered by tuition—the part that comes from students and their families—has more than doubled. If those proportions had remained the same—if we had continued to hold up our end—tuitions would be less than half of what they are, with all that that implies for student debt.

The system isn't unsustainable, as someone recently remarked; it isn't being sustained. Now we're talking about college-by-MOOC and the $10K BA. Public higher education is going the way of so many other public programs: starved of funds, then blamed for failing to deliver. We inherited a strong and flourishing country, and instead of making the investments—that is, the sacrifices—to maintain it, we chose to suck it dry and stick our children with the bill. If you want to see who is to blame for student debt, just look in the mirror. And if parents find themselves supporting kids beyond their college years, that is only, in the aggregate, a form of compensatory justice: the intergenerational transfer of wealth that should have been effected through taxation.

Yet if we're going to create a genuinely fair society, we'll need to do still more than pay for free, first-rate public higher education. For kids to have an equal chance in college, they need to get an equal chance before they get there. Some level of inequality is inevitable; some people are always going to do better than others. The key is to prevent that inequality from being handed down. That doesn't mean that every child must have the same; it simply means that every one must have enough. Above all, it means eliminating inequality in K–12. We know what that would take, the one reform that almost no one in authority wants to see enacted: equalizing funding nationwide. Even better, giving lower-income children *more*, to balance out inequities at home, as they do in countries with the best educational systems, like Finland, Canada, and Singapore. Either course would entail funding schools out of general revenue rather than primarily through local property taxes. The former is what most developed countries do. The latter, by design, is a way for the affluent to perpetuate their privilege.

All this, of course, would take a lot of money. Fortunately, we have a lot of money; we just spend it on the wrong things. "We're broke," you often hear. No, actually, we're not. Even on a per capita basis, we are still, with a few small exceptions, the richest country in the world. We need to tame the $700 billion gorilla of defense, defeat the prison lobby in the states, and raise a lot more money. Corporate taxes as a share of federal revenue are less than half of what they were before the 1980s. If businesses want workers who are better trained, they're going to have to help the rest of us to pay for them. As for the famous 1 percent, their slice of the national income, which stayed at about 10 percent from 1953 to 1981, has risen to about 23 percent. In a $16 trillion economy, the difference represents a premium of more than $2 trillion a year, about four times the federal deficit. As far as I'm concerned, that money belongs to the rest of us. By manipulating the legislative and legal systems—which is to say, by buying them—the rich have simply stolen it.

But taxes aren't the only issue, and the super-wealthy aren't the only ones who've benefited from our ever-growing inequality. The top percentile's share is higher than at almost any time since 1928, but the share that accrues to the top 10 percent has risen to its highest level ever (or at least since 1913, the year that record keeping started), more than 50 percent. The fact is that "the 1 percent," as a concept and slogan, is a very convenient way for the upper middle class, the rest of the elite—the people, by and large, who went to selective colleges and who plan to send their kids in turn—to let themselves off the hook.

Starving public education, higher and otherwise, doesn't benefit them only in the form of lower taxes. It also rigs the economic system for their children. Take most of the kids out of line, and yours are going to get a whole lot more. That's the dirty little secret no one in the upper middle class, which has come to display a kind of Victorian engorgement with its own virtue, is willing to talk about. We all believe, or claim to believe, in social mobility, but we also all know, in our heart of hearts, that social mobility is a zero-sum game. For every person who climbs up the income distribution, someone else falls down. The kind of individuals who go to elite colleges, Caitlin Flanagan remarks, are enlightened enough to be politically correct, but not enough to "find the very idea of an elite college objectionable." We preen ourselves on our progressive views on race, gender, and sexuality, but we blind ourselves to the social division that matters the most, that we guard most jealously, that forms the basis of our comfort, our self-respect, and even of our virtue itself: class.

It comes to this: the elite have purchased self-perpetuation at the price of their children's happiness. The more hoops kids have to jump through, the more it costs to get them through them and the fewer families can do it. But the more they have to jump through, the more miserable they are. Everything we looked at in the first part of this book—the panic, the exhaustion, the sense of emptiness and aimlessness, the fearfulness and cynicism—as well as everything we've looked at in the final part—the entitlement, the mediocrity, the cluelessness that comes of social segregation, the spectacular failure of leadership—is the inevitable outcome of the elite's attempt to privilege their children to the detriment of everybody else's. It is a kind of nemesis or tragic retribution. You think you're screwing other people's kids, but you also end up fucking up your own.

Self-overcoming is a serious business. It has nothing in common with "service," which may be thought of as the charity you give to people after you've impoverished them. You want to help the less fortunate? Get out of their way. In other words, stop hogging all the resources. Social justice means you give up some of what you have so others can have more. That is finally the issue that confronts us as we think about higher education in this country. Are we going to remain a winner-take-all society? Will we continue to maintain an artificial scarcity of educational resources, then drive our children into terror and despair by making them compete with one another for the spaces that are left? Will we insist on squandering the lion's share of our collective human capital instead of mobilizing everybody's talent for the greater good? Are we devolving from a republic into a society of clans, a world where every family withdraws behind its walls and lets the commons fall to ruin?

In *Jude the Obscure,* Thomas Hardy wrote the story of a poor, brilliant, hardworking boy who is denied the chance to rise in life when he is blocked from entering an elite university. Years later, another boy appears at his doorstep—perhaps his own, perhaps somebody else's. Will he take him in? This is what he finally decides:

> *The beggarly question of parentage—what is it, after all? What does it matter, when you come to think about it, whether a child is yours by blood or not? All the little ones of our time are collectively the children of us adults of the time, and entitled to our general care.*

If we are to create a decent society, a just society, a wise and prosperous society, a society where children can learn for the love of learning and people can work for the love of work, then that is what we must believe. We don't have to love our neighbors as ourselves, but we need to love our neighbor's children as our own. We have tried aristocracy. We have tried meritocracy. Now it's time to try democracy.

# Acknowledgments

This book is truly a collective effort. To thank all those who've helped me with the project, since before it even was a project, I would need to enumerate everyone who has written in response to one of my articles, asked a question at a campus event, or taken a class I visited—not to mention everyone I taught as a professor. I hope this book itself provides a form of thanks.

My highest gratitude goes to the many former students who have shared their insights and experiences over the years, especially Laura Zax, Ed Goode, Su Ching Teh, Nikki Greenwood, Alex Milsom, Matt Strother, Joanna Neborsky, Krista Deitemeyer, Aaron Thier, Chiara Scully, Amy Fish, Nicole Allan, Mariangela Crema, Alex Schwartz, Rachel Mannheimer, David Gorin, Curt Ellis, Molly Worthen, Kate Riley, Blake Charlton, Emma Vawter, Adrian Quinlan, Benita Singh, Maria Richardson, Jasper Sherman-Presser, John McEachin, Presca Ahn, David Busis, Jinan Joudeh, Al Kegel, Maria

Spiegel, Chrissie Schmidt, Catherine Killingsworth, and Sabrina Silver. Thanks also to Matt, Helen Rittlemeyer, and Ben Orlin for permission to quote from unpublished essays.

Fond thanks to the friends and former colleagues with whom I have batted these issues around, especially Blakey Vermeule, Sarah Mahurin, Ravit Reichman, Wes Davis, Pericles Lewis, Barry McCrea, Priscilla Gilman, and Donald Brown. Others who have offered valuable dialogue include Tammy Kim, Rob Reich, Mark Edmundson, Lloyd Thacker, Lara Galinsky, Gloria Kweskin, Becko Copenhaver, Kathy Kirshenbaum, Amy Whitaker, Caroline Kahn, Jonathan Weiler, Daniel Schwartz, Frances Bronet, William Treseder, Ronald Newburgh, Josipa Roksa, Dan Chazan, Stephen Bergman, Yong Zhao, Herman D'Hooge, and Michael Koehn.

For research help, thanks to Terri Lobdell, James Axtell, Roger Geiger, Gurumurthy Neelakantan, D. Parthasarathy, Sean F. Reardon, Dorothe J. Bach, Chris Miller, Gong Szeto, and the ever-gracious Andrew Delbanco.

Thanks especially to the people who have made my campus and other appearances possible, including Lily Janiak at Yale's St. Anthony Hall; Lois Beckett and Elsa Kim at the student committee of the Harvard Humanities Center; Jefferson Cowie at Cornell; Colonel Scott Krawczyk, Karin Roffman, and Elizabeth Samet at West Point; Blakey Vermeule and Jennifer Summit at Stanford; Julius Taranto at the Pomona College Student Union; Peter Upham at the Association of Boarding Schools; the students at the McCoy Center for Ethics in Society at Stanford; George Karnezis at Portland State; Douglass Sullivan-González at the Honors College of the University of Mississippi; Mary Collins at Central Connecticut; David McGlynn and Timothy Spurgin at Lawrence; Logan Spangler at the Business Ethics Society of the University of Virginia; Bryan Garsten at Yale-NUS; Marc DeWitt at the Y Syndicate; David Schiller and Jessica

Levenstein at Horace Mann; Saahil Abhijit Desai at the Associated Students of Pomona College; Gayle Greene at Scripps; Larry and Claudia Allums at the Dallas Institute of Humanities and Culture; as well as their peers, colleagues, and support staff. Special thanks to Audrey Bilger and the many others at Claremont McKenna, where I finalized the manuscript, and engaged in much enriching conversation, during a residency last fall.

Titanic thanks to Robert Wilson at the *American Scholar*, who offered shelter to a cranky little essay after it was orphaned by a wealthy publication, and who has continued to publish my thoughts on these matters ever since. Thanks also to John Palattella at the *Nation* and Evan Goldstein at the *Chronicle of Higher Education* for additional opportunities to vent my spleen about the state of college in America. Thanks to my editor Alessandra Bastagli, as well as to the staff at Free Press, to Alex Jacobs, Tyler Allen, and the rest of the people at Cheney Literary, and most of all, to my knight in shining armor and agent extraordinaire, Elyse Cheney, without whom I'd be standing by an I-5 exit ramp, holding a sign that said "Will Profess for $."

For her insight, her wisdom, her patience, and her wicked sense of humor, my deepest gratitude goes to my wife, Aleeza Jill Nussbaum: in conversation and in life, a true partner.

Lastly, thanks to everyone who gave permission to quote from emails or spoken remarks on condition of anonymity. A few details have been changed to protect identities. Typographical errors have been silently corrected and material redacted without ellipses, but in no case have meanings been altered.

**For source notes and suggestions** for further reading, go to excellent sheep.com.

# About the Author

William Deresiewicz was a professor of English at Yale for ten years and a graduate instructor at Columbia, where he also went to college, for five. His essay "The Disadvantages of an Elite Education" has been viewed more than one million times online. A frequent speaker on college campuses, he is also a prominent cultural critic whose work has appeared in the *New York Times,* the *Atlantic,* the *Nation,* the *New Republic,* and many other publications. He is the author of *A Jane Austen Education: How Six Novels Taught Me About Love, Friendship, and the Things That Really Matter.*